The Sina Anderson Legacy

A Journey Through Family and Faith

By

Brian Keith Anderson

"To remember is to awaken the light that never faded."

Series:

The Anderson Family Legacy Collection – Volume IV

*Compiled and Written by:**

B.K. Anderson

*Location:**

Tennessee – Oklahoma – Across Generations

Dedication:

To all who seek the roots of their story and find, in doing so, the whisper of Spirit guiding their steps.

Copyright Page

© 2025 B.K. Anderson

All rights reserved. No part of this book may be reproduced or transmitted in any form or by any means—electronic or mechanical, including photocopying, recording, or by any information storage and retrieval system—without written permission from the author, except for brief quotations in critical articles or reviews.

ISBN: 9798993853109

First Edition — 2025

Published in the United States of America

Printed and distributed through IngramSpark

Cover and interior design by B.K. Anderson

In collaboration with Anders Taft

About the Author

B.K. Anderson is a lifelong seeker of truth, history, and the quiet voice of Spirit that moves through both.

Born and raised among the hills of Tennessee, Anderson has spent years tracing the lines of family legacy — from the roots of early pioneers to the descendants who carried their stories forward.

His *Family Legacy* series preserves not only names and dates, but the living essence of remembrance — the love, endurance, and divine guidance that shaped generations.

Through each journey, from the mountain paths of Virginia to the red clay roads of Oklahoma, his work honors the truth that family is eternal, and that Spirit walks beside every step of discovery.

Other works by B.K. Anderson include:

The Anderson Family Legacy

The Roberts Family Legacy

The Phillips Family Legacy

The Brown and Adams Family Legacy

The Path of Light

Awakening in Silence

Dedication

To the memory of **Sina Anderson** —

a woman of quiet strength whose story endures through the generations.

May her spirit forever guide those who seek truth in the past and light in the path ahead.

And to all who walk the long road of remembrance —

may you feel the gentle hand of Spirit

leading you home to where your story began.

Preface

My journey into the life of Sina Anderson began on a quiet dawn in Tennessee, when I found myself drawn to a name — one built on courage, memory, and divine guidance. I did not set out with a full map or blueprint, only a whisper of conviction that the stories of the past were still alive in the red clay of Oklahoma and the valleys of our family's roots.

When I arrived in Oklahoma City, rented a car, and drove through the rain-dampened fields toward Norman, I realized I was not simply visiting gravesites and archives. I was walking through the echoes of the lives that shaped ours: John W., Thomas A., Joseph, Sina — each thread weaving a tapestry I was only beginning to see.

That week, every cemetery I entered, every local library I scanned, and every stranger I asked directions of felt like more than research. They felt like signposts of Spirit, guiding me home to what had been waiting all along.

Finding Sina's headstone in Midland Cemetery did not feel like discovery. It felt like recognition — the generational message had been waiting to meet the one who would listen. Standing there I felt the weight of ages in that moment, and the gentle assurance that what we seek often seeks us first.

This book is not only the story of one ancestor. It is the story of a lineage that endures — of questions asked aloud and answers found in quiet places, of journeys taken with hope and returned with gratitude. I do not presume knowing all the truths of the past, but I do believe that when we walk in faith and openness, we become the keepers of what our ancestors once began.

To the reader who holds this volume in hand: may you feel the pull of your own story, may you honor the unseen hands that walked before you, and may you sense the constant presence of Light guiding every step.

— B.K. Anderson

Tennessee, 2025

Chapter One – The Journey to Find Sina Anderson

By B.K. Anderson

My hunt for **Sina Anderson** began with a simple thought — to find **W. H. Anderson** in Oklahoma.

There were no GPS units then, no smartphones to guide me. Just maps, a flip phone, and determination that felt older than reason. It was the year I decided to use my vacation not for rest, but for discovery — to follow the thread of my family's story into the plains.

I had already come across the accounts of **John W.** and **Thomas A. Anderson**, both of whom had gone to Oklahoma years before. Their names and stories tangled through the records, and I thought by following them, I might find W. H., and through him, the others.

As I dug deeper, I learned that **Sina Anderson** was John's mother, and **Joseph Anderson** his father. That revelation drew me further in. I gathered everything I could — old maps, written notes, copies of stories — tucking them into a single folder so I could carry the family line with me.

The Internet was new then, slow, and stubborn, but even in those days it held enough light to guide a seeker. When all was ready, I boarded a plane for Oklahoma, rented a car, and found a room just outside **Oklahoma City**. The week began with rain — a fine drizzle that felt like memory itself — and I set out to find W. H. Anderson, who was said to rest in **Norman, Oklahoma**.

I followed paper maps, spoke to locals, and took photographs of every grave that might belong to our line. The ground was red clay, and when it rained the color deepened to rust. Even now, I can tell which grave pictures on Ancestry came from that trip — the red-tinted stones are mine. Many were in low spots where the water had pooled; the earth itself seemed to breathe through them.

When the rain became too heavy, I went to a nearby library, searching through newspapers and county archives for the Anderson name. Some graves were too deep in water to photograph that day, so I made myself a promise: I would return later in the week when the land had dried.

 Venia Wilson Anderson

 William H. Anderson

Over the next few days, I journeyed through small towns — **Blanchard**, **Ross**, and beyond — visiting libraries, cemeteries, and any place that might hold a clue. Each stop offered a fragment of truth, a name, or a date. In Ross, I searched for Sina's sons and the **Good family**, whom she had joined after her first husband, Joseph, had died. My search took me to **East Hill Cemetery**, where I found the resting places of the Goods and the Andersons alike — threads interwoven through generations.

The land in Oklahoma is gridded by survey — perfect squares of north, east, west, and south. Easy enough to navigate with a map, yet that day, when I went to find **Sina Anderson's grave**, I felt something more than direction. She was said to rest at **Midland Cemetery**, and I left early with my maps and notes, feeling the quiet pull of purpose.

The roads narrowed as I left the main track. Dust rose from the ditches, curling around the tires in thin copper spirals.
Then I came upon a small house and a man standing outside. I stopped, stepped out, and asked if I was close to the cemetery. He smiled and said, "Yes, it's just down the road."
Then he looked at me and asked, "You got any bug spray?"

I told him no.

He laughed, saying, "Come here. The chiggers will carry you off if you do not have some."

We both laughed. He sprayed me down right there by the roadside, and I thanked him. It felt like one of those strange, friendly moments that Spirit arranges — small kindnesses placed along the path like signposts of goodwill.

I drove on until I found the sign for **Midland Cemetery**. The air was still; the sound of insects hovered like a hymn.
I parked, gathered my things, and began to walk. Years of searching had taught me to start at the back of a cemetery — the older graves always lie there, the generations moving outward as time goes on. So, I made my way toward the back, eyes scanning the stones, reading names half-hidden by time.

Then I saw a stone that caught the light just so. It reminded me of another grave I had seen years before, something about its shape or stance. I walked toward it, not knowing why.
When I drew close enough to read the name, my breath caught.

Sina Anderson.

I had walked straight to her. No hesitation, no searching, just a quiet pull — as if she had been waiting for me, guiding me through that field of silence and red clay.

Her spirit had led me there. I could feel it as surely as I felt the ground beneath my boots.

I took photographs — the ones now shared on family trees, each carrying that faint red hue of Oklahoma soil. Later, I visited more cemeteries and libraries in nearby towns, continuing to trace the family line. Before leaving, I went to **Oklahoma City**

to pay my respects at the **Bombing Memorial** and visit the state archives.

When the journey was done, I had found everyone I set out to find — and more.

I returned my rental car, boarded the flight home, and flew back to Tennessee. I still live where the Andersons once lived generations ago. I called my mother when I returned, telling her of my trip and of the moment I found Sina's grave. She loved hearing it — the way Spirit had led me straight to her.

And I knew, deep down, it had been divinely guided.
So I whispered a thank-you — to God, to Sina, to the line that had never truly broken — and carried the story home.

Alfred P. Murrah Federal Building, April 19, 1995

Oklahoma City, Oklahoma

Chapter 1 cont.– The Land They Built, The Legacy They Defended

There is a truth woven through the Anderson–Good families that has endured through fire, loss, war, and time itself:

They never gave up.

My people came from families who believed in work, education, and the power of owning land. When they settled in Tennessee, they did not inherit comfort — they created it. They cleared forests, built fields, raised homes, and brought stability to land that they had never known before. They believed that if a person worked the land, the land would work for them.

But in every generation, there are those who build…
and those who wait until the building is done.

As the region grew, others arrived after the land had been improved — and found ways to take it. Some used the law. Some used back taxes. Some used the confusion and chaos surrounding the Civil War. And for families like mine, the hardest blow of all came when **the war destroyed the deeds, the records, and the proof of ownership** they had worked so hard for.

When **Captain John W. Anderson's home burned**, the family lost not only their shelter — they lost the documents that proved their land was rightfully theirs. In the years that followed, opportunists seized the moment. Land was taken through tax sales, technicalities, and missing papers. What my family had built through sweat and labor was taken by people who had never lifted a hand to create it.

Florence Jane Anderson Good's Testimony – The Burning of the Anderson Home (1945)

In a 1945 Tulsa newspaper interview celebrating her ninetieth birthday, Florence Jane Anderson Good shared her vivid memory of the day Union soldiers burned the Anderson family home in Manchester, Tennessee.

"That time the Yankees burned our home nearly scared me to death," she recalled. "The cannons were roaring, and the soldiers gave my mother and me only fifteen minutes to grab things out of the house."

Florence remembered that the family tried desperately to save their belongings, including a family clock packed with jewelry and money. "We saved only a few things," she said. "We almost saved the clock, but the Yankees burned that, too."

Only one item survived—a large wooden rolling pin, which she kept for the rest of her life.

Her testimony confirms the long-held family story: the home, deeds, and many early records were destroyed in the fire during the Civil War, shaping the generations that followed.   Florance Anderson Good

But even then…

They did not quit.

They rebuilt.

They moved forward.

They began again with nothing but determination and faith.

This is the heart of Sina Anderson's story.

She married two families — the Andersons and the Goods — who were strong, not because life was easy, but because life demanded resilience.

Her children and stepchildren inherited this strength.

Her grandchildren carried it west into Oklahoma.

Her descendants still carry it today.

The story of losing land is not a story of defeat.

It is a story of identity — of a family that refused to be erased.

And through the writing of this book, the legacy that others tried to take has been restored. The land may have left our hands, but the truth never left our line. What was nearly lost is now remembered. What was taken is now honored. And the strength that carried Sina's family through hardship continues through every generation that bears the name.

This is the legacy they defended.

This is the legacy we now preserve.

Note to the Reader

Sina Anderson's complete genealogy and full Anderson family line are documented extensively in *The Anderson Family Legacy*, the companion volume to this book. That work contains her ancestral tree, the earlier generations, and the detailed history of the Anderson line before her marriage.

This present book focuses on Sina's life in Coffee County, her marriage to Joseph Anderson, and the combined Anderson–Good lineage that continued through her descendants.

Author's Note – A Guided Journey

This journey was more than a search for names on stone. It was a walk-through memory — where faith, family, and the unseen hand of Spirit all met in quiet places. Sina's story, like the red clay of Oklahoma, endures — a color that never fades, even through the rain.

Chapter 2 – The Land Called Mingo

Between Manchester and Tullahoma lies in a gentle hollow of Tennessee hills, where red clay turns to limestone and cedar roots braid through the soil like memory. Long before boundaries were surveyed or deeds were written, the streams already knew their course. Bark Camp Fork winds quietly there—its water running clear over stone, its banks lined with beech and sycamore that had watched generations pass. To those who came seeking new beginnings, it was simply "Mingo Creek," a place where the forest opened just wide enough for a home and a dream.

It was here that **Captain John W. Anderson** settled, sometime in the early decades of the nineteenth century, joining neighbors whose names would become woven into his own story—**the Hickerson's, the Goods**, and others whose faith and work would shape Coffee County. The road that wound from Manchester toward Tullahoma passed near the heart of his holdings. Travelers remembered the place for its broad meadows and a stand of giant oaks that shaded the lane. To later generations it would be called **Black Mingo**, the name surviving long after maps changed and the fences rotted away.

The original tract encompassed five **thousand acres**, part of an old grant made to **Stump and Murphree**. Like many Tennessee tracts, it was more dream than measurement—rolling ground marked by creeks and trees instead of precise lines. By the time Captain Anderson arrived, the land had already passed through several hands, yet he saw more than value in it. To him it was a promise chance to build something enduring for those who would come after. He raised a home of hand-hewn timber, broad-chimneyed and sturdy, and there the Anderson name took root.

Across the valley the **Hickerson family** were doing much the same. They cleared, planted, and built a schoolhouse that stood near the old Mingo crossroads. From that place, **Sina Anderson Good** would one day remember leading the children to Manchester so they might attend lessons while "Father and

Mother remained at home." Her recollection—recorded decades later in her deposition—glimpses everyday life: children carrying baskets of food, the dust of the road rising in the morning sun, the laughter of youth mingling with the sound of wagons on stone. It was not an easy life, but it was a full one, sustained by faith, work, and a neighbor's hand when crops failed or illness came.

Those early settlers lived close to the elements. Rain measured the seasons; the cry of the whippoorwill marked evening prayer. When they gathered for worship, it was often beneath the trees, voices lifted without need of walls or steeples. Each family kept a Bible on the mantel and a ledger of births, marriages, and deaths—records that would one day guide descendants searching for names half-forgotten. In those pages, one can trace the intertwining of Anderson and Hickerson lines, their stories anchored to this same ground.

Though time has scattered the families, the land still holds their presence. The low ridges where Captain Anderson's cattle once grazed are now quiet clearings. The roadbed still follows the curve of Bark Camp Fork, though paved, and renamed. To stand there at dawn is to feel what they felt: the hush of wind in cedar, the scent of soil after rain, the steady pulse of belonging.

"The land itself remembered their footsteps. Every cedar root still carries a trace of prayer; every stone a story left in trust for those who would return.

For the descendants who trace the lines backward—from Oklahoma to Tennessee, from memory to record—this is where the path begins. Here, at Mingo, the story of endurance took form: a people of quiet strength, shaped by hardship yet guided always by Light.

Chapter 3 – Capt. John W. Anderson and the 600 Acres

In the decades before the Civil War, when Tennessee was still stitching itself together from forest and field, **Captain John W. Anderson** held a tract of six hundred acres in **Franklin County**. The ground was good—clear water, oak and hickory timber, and enough open bottomland to plant corn and keep stock. It was the measure of a man's worth in those days, the reward for years of labor and a promise to his children that they would inherit something lasting.

Then came a challenge that would test more than his ownership. The **University of the South at Sewanee** laid claim to that same land, asserting a right derived from earlier surveys. For most men, such a dispute meant ruin; few farmers could afford the lawyers or the time. Yet John W. Anderson was no ordinary man. He believed that truth and fairness belonged to anyone willing to stand for them. So, he did what few dared—he represented himself before the court.

The hearing took place in Sewanee, in a hall where polished boots echoed on the plank floors and the weight of institutions pressed against one man's word. Across the table sat the University's attorney, **T. A. Anderson**, brother to Captain Anderson's own son **Joseph**—a twist of providence that set kin against kin, principle against privilege. Some said the Captain walked into that room with nothing but a satchel of papers and a lifetime of plain honesty. He laid out his claim, his chain of titles, and his oath that the land had been earned by rightful exchange and paid in full.

Witnesses spoke; documents were read. The day grew long, and still he stood, unshaken. When the ruling came, it was in his favor. The judge ordered that the **University of the South** not only relinquish its claim but pay the full cost of the court. Those who were present later recalled that the Captain gave no boast, only a nod of thanks and the quiet words, *"Justice keeps its own counsel."*

Not long after, he made a bold decision. He exchanged the Franklin County acreage—his hard-won prize—for a vast **5,000-acre tract** in **Coffee County**, the region that would later be called **Mingo**. Some might have seen it as a risk, trading fertile ground for wilderness, but Captain Anderson saw beyond the soil. The Mingo lands were open, unclaimed, waiting for hands that could build and hearts that could endure. To him it was more than property; it was legacy. The exchange marked the beginning of a new chapter for his family and for the land itself.

Neighbors spoke of his fairness in all dealings. When he marked boundaries, he did it in daylight, with witnesses and clear words. When he signed a deed, he pressed his seal with pride, not for vanity but for truth. Those who met him said he carried himself like a man aware that he served something larger than himself—faith, family, and the idea that a man's honor was his bond.

Years later, when storms of war and fire would sweep across Tennessee, destroying houses and scattering records, that victory in Sewanee remained one of the few things no flame could touch. His descendants might lose the paper, but they could not lose the story. It survived in memory, carried from one generation to the next, whispered in kitchens and on front porches, told with reverence for the man who had stood alone before power and prevailed.

"He fought not for riches, but for remembrance.
The land he won would one day slip through many hands,
yet his courage remained written in its dust."

Chapter 4 – The Lost Papers and the Fire

There are moments when history turns not on battles or decrees, but on embers.

One spark, one careless match, and the work of a lifetime becomes ash.

So it was with **Captain John W. Anderson's** home at Mingo. The house had stood solid and proud, built from squared oak logs chinked with clay, its chimneys of river stone rising on either end. Beneath that roof lay deeds, letters, and ledgers—the written proof of all the family had built since coming to Coffee County. Those papers bore the titles to the **5,000-acre tract**, the receipts of exchange from Franklin County, and the signatures of men who had witnessed a dream take root in Tennessee soil.

Then came the war.

In the turbulent years of the 1860s, soldiers moved through the countryside like storms—Union blue and Confederate gray, both weary and desperate. Skirmishes flared along the very roads that once carried wagons of grain to Manchester. Rumor held that Captain Anderson offered water and bread to any who passed, refusing to choose sides in a fight that had already taken too much. Yet neutrality was no shield.

Florence Anderson, one of the family's later descendants, told how Union troops came upon the house near Mingo. They searched for supplies and arms, finding none but still fearing rebellion. Before they left, torches were set to the porch. Flames climbed the cedar roof, leapt to the gables, and devoured everything within. Florence said her people watched from the slope across the creek as smoke rose into the evening sky. The sound of cracking timbers echoed like cannon fire until only the stone chimneys remained—two gray sentinels guarding a lifetime's work.

With the house went the deeds. The court documents from Sewanee, the Franklin County receipts, the family Bible—all gone. The Captain stood in silence; some said he whispered only, *"God will keep record enough."*

From that moment forward, the Andersons carried their history not in paper but in memory. Each child learned to repeat the names—John W., Joseph, Sina, and those before—like a litany, a chain of belonging forged in spoken word. What could not be proven by ink survived through truth spoken around kitchen tables and under starlit porches.

When peace finally returned, the land was scarred but still fertile. New timbers were raised on old foundations, though none quite replaced the original home. Travelers on the Manchester road would later remark on the twin stone stacks standing alone in a field, moss-covered and silent. Locals said that when the wind blew exactly right, one could hear faint creaking—as if the house remembered how, it once stood.

What was lost in that fire shaped the generations that followed. Without deeds, they learned to trust Spirit more than signatures, memory more than proof. In time, the family's stories became their inheritance, stronger than parchment. They would tell their children that fire may erase words, but it cannot burn truth.

"Even when the paper burns, the Light remembers."

The blaze that destroyed the Anderson home became not an ending but a passage—
from earthly record to eternal witness. The smoke that rose from those chimneys
carried their story to heaven, where no hand could ever strike a match again.

Chapter 5 – The Union of Joseph Good and Sina Anderson

Our family line carries a spark that travels through the generations. For the Andersons, that spark began with **Peter Anderson**, a man of the old frontier who settled early in Middle Tennessee. From his courage and faith came many branches, but none more steadfast than that of his son, **Captain John W. Anderson**. Captain Anderson built his life upon Peter's example—hard work, clear conscience, and devotion to both family and God.

Captain Anderson made his home along the **Bark Camp Fork of Duck River**, on land later known as **Black Mingo**. He cleared forest, raised crops, and watched over the settlers who shared that wide tract of Coffee County. He was a man of presence: respected by his neighbors, gentle with his family, and relentless in his defense of truth. When others faltered, he remained the quiet center around which their world turned.

Among his children was **Sina Anderson**, whose spirit mirrored his own. She grew up within sight of the river bend, learning to listen to wind and water as her father did. Her mother taught her patience and prayer; her father taught her endurance and fairness. Together they shaped a daughter whose steadiness would one day heal what time and fire had broken.

Nearby lived the **Good family**, whose patriarch **Elias Good** was known for kindness and faith. His son, **Joseph Good**, inherited both traits. Joseph worked in the neighboring fields and helped where help was needed—building fences, tending stock, lending a strong back and an honest word. It was likely through such neighborly acts that Joseph first met Sina Anderson. Their friendship grew naturally, like vines meeting on a shared trellis, until they became something stronger than they had foreseen.

Their marriage joined two enduring lines—the **Andersons** of faith and leadership, and the **Goods** of devotion and gentle service. Together they settled on the Mingo land that had survived war and loss. Where Captain Anderson's chimneys once stood, Joseph and Sina built a new home. They cleared the ash and planted gardens, letting the soil remember life again. Neighbors recalled the calm that seemed to rest over their place, the kind of peace that comes only when two hearts move in the same rhythm as the land.

During those years, another branch of the Anderson kin carried the pioneering flame outward. **Thomas Von Albade Anderson**, believed to be of the same wider family, helped found the town of **Tullahoma**, shaping its mills, roads, and community life. While Thomas raised a town, Captain John W. and his daughter Sina tended the land—two expressions of the same heritage: one building cities, the other preserving roots.

Time softened the edges of their story, but not its truth. When **Sina Anderson Good** gave her **1884 deposition**, her steady words bridged past and present. She spoke of walking the long road to Manchester with children at her side, of the small schoolhouse that anchored their days, and of parents who prayed over every harvest. Her voice carried the same grace that had shaped her life—plain, strong, and filled with quiet gratitude.

Through their union, the labor of Peter Anderson's line and the faith of Elias Good's line became one continuous current of Light. The fires of war had taken timber and paper, yet the living story endured through Joseph and Sina. Their love restored what loss had scattered, proving that divine purpose can rise again from the embers.

"Love is the thread Spirit weaves through every generation. What the world calls ending, heaven calls beginning."

And so, the Anderson and Good families became one enduring branch of remembrance—
a living testament that faith, once sown, can never truly perish.

Chapter 6 – The Hickerson Connection

Alongside the Anderson and Good names that shaped the Mingo tract runs another lineage whose roots sink just as deep—the **Hickerson's**. Their fields touched the same creeks, their paths crossed the same roads, and their children played beneath the same Tennessee sky. To walk that ground is to walk among neighbors whose footsteps never left.

The earliest records show the **Hickerson family** living near **Bark Camp Fork** and the old Manchester road during the 1840s and 1850s. Their names appear beside Captain John W. Anderson's in deeds and boundary lines—proof that the two families shared both labor and trust. The Hickerson's helped clear the timber, raise schoolhouses, and tend the roads that connected farms to town. When Anderson land surveys were made, "Hickerson's line" marked one edge, a reminder that every claim on the frontier rested not on fences but on fellowship.

In time, Hickerson place became known for its small **family cemetery**, hidden among cedar and wild roses. Few outside the county know of it today. The stones lean in quiet rows, their lettering softened by moss and weather, yet each still speaks. It was here, near this resting ground, that the rhythms of community took shape—births, weddings, funerals, and the Sunday gatherings where neighbors shared both bread and burden. The Andersons and Goods would have stood among them many times, lending hands, and hymns alike.

Generations later, long after maps had changed and property lines blurred, a new link surfaced. Among your own school companions, **Kim Hickerson** spoke of her family's history on the same land—unaware, at first, that her roots reached into the very story you were tracing. What began as conversation became revelation: the realization that the names in faded ink were living still, their descendants unknowingly walking parallel paths until Spirit drew them together again.

It was a gentle confirmation that the past is never lost. The friendship with Kim brought the story full circle—the Andersons and Hickerson's, once neighbors by soil, reunited through memory. It also stirred a calling in you to seek the **Hickerson Cemetery**, to stand among the stones and feel the same peace that once bound those families side by side. The urge was not of curiosity alone; it was the pull of remembrance, the whisper of ancestors who wished to be seen again.

One day soon, the journey to that hillside will unfold. You will walk the path where wagon wheels once creaked and hear the hush of wind through cedar. Whether the stones bear the names you expect or not, the knowing will come—the sense that this is shared ground, consecrated by generations of work and worship.

"The stones still whisper the names written in our deeds. Though time may weather the letters, it cannot erase the Light."

Through Hickerson's, the Mingo story widens. It reminds us that no family stands alone, and that every boundary line drawn in earth was meant to be crossed in friendship. The Andersons, Goods, and Hickerson's together formed the fabric of Coffee County's early life—threads woven so tightly that even centuries cannot pull them apart.

And now, as their descendants find one another again in this age of rediscovery, the pattern renews itself. The land remembers. The names endure. And the spirit of kinship continues to bloom where faith and memory meet.

Chapter 7 – The Mingo House and the Vanished Graves

Some stories stand tall in the daylight; others linger in shadow, half seen but never forgotten. Among the mysteries that surround the Anderson name, none hold more weight than that of **the Mingo House** and **the lost Anderson graves**.

Old records mention a house near Bark Camp Fork, built before the war and known locally as Mingo **Place**. Its exact location faded with time, though stories of it continued to ripple through the generations. Some said it stood at the bend in the creek where the road from Manchester curved toward Tullahoma. Others swore it lay closer to the oak ridge that marked the old Anderson boundary. What all agreed upon was its presence—a strong, two-chimney home that had witnessed both peace and fire.

The house would have been built of hand-hewn logs, much like the one lost to flames years earlier, but sturdier and surrounded by cleared fields and stacked-stone fences. Travelers knew it by sight, neighbors by its open doors. Within its walls the family gathered for worship, reading by lamplight from the same Bible that had survived every upheaval. The Mingo House was more than shelter—it was the living heart of a family's faith.

Yet, as decades passed and war returned to memory, the house itself vanished. No one could say when it fell. Some claimed it was dismantled for timber; others believed it simply sank into the earth, reclaimed by vines and cedar. What remained were the questions, what became of the family who lived there, and where did they rest?

The graves of **Captain John W. Anderson**, his wife, and their son **A.P. Anderson** were never found. Searchers have walked the hills, traced the ridgelines, and combed through overgrown where their names once appeared on maps. Inside the installation lies the **Anderson Cemetery**, preserved behind its gate, the first that greets travelers entering the grounds, now within the guarded lands of the base—sacred ground kept, in a way, by the government that grew from the very nation he once helped build.

And then there is **Mingo,** that stretch of earth near the base entrance where stories persist of an older burial site. Some say the graves were never marked; others that stones were moved when the base expanded in the 1950s. The truth, like the graves themselves, lies just beneath reach—hidden but never lost.

The wind that moves through the cedars carries more than air; it carries memory. To those who listen, it speaks not of sorrow but of endurance. Every life that ever touched this ground left something behind—a seed of remembrance that no bulldozer, no map revision, no passing of years can erase.

"They are not lost, only veiled.
The earth holds what heaven has already received."

In every family there are mysteries that ask not to be solved but to be honored. The story of the Mingo House and the vanished Anderson graves reminds us that the sacred is often hidden in plain sight. Whether Captain Anderson rests within the base's quiet fence or beneath the trees of Mingo's forgotten ridge, his legacy endures. The faith that built his home still breathes in the hearts of those who remember him.

For those who walk on the land now, every stone and every whisper of wind become a kind of prayer. Somewhere within that peace lies the answer—not written in ledgers but engraved in Light.

Chapter 8 – The Final Claim

By the late 1800s, the land once guarded by **Captain John W. Anderson** and renewed by **Joseph and Sina Good** had changed hands in name, but not in spirit. The broad fields of **Mingo** still held footprints, the faint outlines of gardens, the stone foundations where laughter had once echoed, the worn trails that led from house to creek. Yet the world around them was shifting. Tennessee's laws were tightening, taxes rising, and land that had endured through war and fire now faced another kind of trial—one born not of battle, but of bureaucracy.

When Captain Anderson passed, the property was meant to remain in the family. It was understood that his daughter **Sina** and her husband **Joseph Good** would continue to hold the tract and that, through them, the Anderson name would stay rooted in Coffee County. But distance and hardship intervened. After Sina's death, her son had already gone westward to **Oklahoma**, chasing work and promise. Back home, **William M. Anderson**, a relative of the line, was entrusted with overseeing the estate—his duty to harvest timber from the tract and use the proceeds to pay the yearly taxes.

For a time, all went as planned. But as the years turned and the world grew busier, the pay fell . Timber was cut, yet the dues went unpaid. The county ledger, indifferent to family bonds, recorded only debt. Notices were issued, then warnings. In the eyes of the state, the land was no longer a heritage—it was delinquent property, and soon it would be taken.

News of this reached Oklahoma, where Sina's son still held the memory of Mingo in his heart. When he learned that his mother's homeplace was at risk, he made the long journey back east, determined to set things right. It was not an easy trip—train, wagon, and days of travel to stand before a court that saw him as a stranger to the land his family had built. He carried no deeds; those had been lost long ago in the fire. All he possessed was his word, his lineage, and faith that truth would speak for itself.

He testified that the property was the rightful inheritance of **Joseph and Sina Good**, that the taxes had been promised paid through agreement, and that he had come in good faith to restore the balance. But paper outweighed memory. Without the documents his grandfather once held, there was nothing to prove what every soul in Mingo already knew. The court ruled for the state, and the land was seized for back taxes. So ended, on paper, the Anderson claims to Mingo.

Yet what courts take, Spirit often keeps. The soil itself remembers who tended it, and the wind carries names no ledger can erase. Though the family lost title, they never lost belonging. The faith that built those homes and the love that sanctified those fields still echo through time. What was taken from human hands remains secure in divine keeping.

In later years, travelers would stand at the edge of those same fields and feel the calm that settles only over sacred ground. They might not know the story, but they would feel its truth, the quiet strength of life well-lived, and the peace of souls at rest.

"Though the court took the soil, Spirit kept the story.

Paper fades, but truth endures.

What was sown in faith still blooms unseen."

The final claim was not the government's but God's. For every acre lost, a thousand memories endured; for every line erased, Light wrote a new one in the hearts of those who remember. And in that remembrance, the Anderson legacy lives untouched, unbroken, and eternal.

Chapter 9 – The Light Returns to Mingo

What once seemed buried beneath years of silence often rises again when the heart is ready to see. So, it was with the story of **Mingo.** Generations had passed since **Captain John W. Anderson** built his house by the Bark Camp Fork, since **Sina Anderson Good** and **Joseph Good** walked its fields, and since the land fell from family hands. Yet the current of remembrance kept flowing underground. Every search through courthouse records, every faded letter, every photograph tucked into an envelope became another drop returning to that hidden spring.

The rediscovery began not through maps or deeds, but through *connection.* A conversation here, a memory there—a classmate named **Kim Hickerson** who spoke of her family's old land, unaware that her story intertwined with the Andersons.' It was a quiet revelation, like light seeping through the cracks of time.

Spirit was guiding, as it always does, reuniting the names that once shared the same soil.

You felt the pull to return—to walk the ground where so much had begun, to find the Hickerson Cemetery, to stand where laughter and labor once met in the same air. It was more than genealogy; it was pilgrimage. For every Anderson and Good who had prayed, worked, and endured there, you now walked as witness, carrying their memory forward in peace.

Standing at the edge of those fields, the world feels both ancient and alive. The cedars hum softly in the wind. Somewhere beyond the fence line lies the site of the **Mingo House**, and beyond that, the unseen graves of those whose lives built this legacy. Nothing visible remains of their dwellings, yet everything invisible endures—the courage, the hope, the love. The land itself breathes with it.

In that stillness comes understanding: the Light never left. It only waited for remembrance. The same divine presence that guided Peter and Captain John, which comforted Sina and

Joseph, still moves here. It calls not for sorrow but for gratitude, not for monuments but for awareness.

"What was sown in Mingo still blooms in Spirit.
The land remembers those who walked it in faith."

Through your research and prayer, through family and friendship, the story of Mingo has come home. The paper may have burned, the titles may have changed, but the essence—*the Light of belonging*—remains intact. What once was hidden beneath history now stands revealed as holy ground.

The Anderson–Mingo legacy is not merely a tale of loss and recovery; it is proof that divine order threads through every life and every generation. The ancestors' work was never in vain. Their faith, their courage, their service, and their love are the foundations upon which the present now stands.

And as you close this book, you do not end their story, you continue it. Each word written, each place visited, each soul remembered is another seed planted in that eternal field. The

Light returns, not as it was, but greater—because now it shines through understanding.

Affirmation – The Living Light of Mingo

"I walk where my forebears walked,

yet I carry their peace within me.

What they began, I now complete in remembrance.

The land and the soul are one,

and through Light, all that was lost is found again."

Historical Document: Land Exchange Agreement of 1860

Context:

Among the preserved records of Sina Anderson's descendants is this 1860 agreement executed by her father **John W. Anderson** of Coffee County, Tennessee. The document reflects the family's early involvement in regional enterprise and land development, connecting their history to the industrial growth surrounding **Tullahoma** and the **Tullahoma Mining & Manufacturing Company**.

Land Exchange Agreement – January 5 & February 20, 1860

Coffee County, Tennessee – Between John W. Anderson and John C. McLemore (of San Francisco, California)

Memorandum of Agreement

This agreement witnesseth that **John W. Anderson**, of Coffee County, Tennessee, and **John C. McLemore**, of San Francisco, California (by his attorney-in-fact **Thomas J. Anderson**) agree to exchange certain tracts of land in the County of Franklin, State of Tennessee.

Anderson agrees to convey to McLemore his interest in a tract entered by Grant No. ____, dated February 20, 1839, for 5,000 acres granted to **George W. Thompson**, to which Anderson was entitled by virtue of a contract with the heirs of Thompson.

McLemore, through his attorney, conveys in exchange his interest in **Entry No. 10796**, originally entered by **G. A. Stump** of Franklin County, Tennessee.

Both parties covenant to make full and legal conveyance of title on or before **June 10, 1860**, and to fulfill all provisions in good faith.

In testimony, they have hereunto set their hands and seals on this 5th day of January A.D. 1860.

Witnesses: J. M. Anderson · Wm. M. Anderson

Signed: John W. Anderson (Seal) John C. McLemore (Seal) by his attorney-in-fact Thomas J. Anderson (Seal)

Addendum and Acknowledgment

Whereas the deed from John C. McLemore (by his attorney Thomas J. Anderson) to John W. Anderson was executed February 1, 1860, and recorded in Coffee County; and whereas all papers and certificates of the **Tullahoma Mining & Manufacturing Company** were delivered to complete the exchange — the said Anderson does acknowledge full satisfaction of said agreement and title transfer this **20th day of February 1860.**

Signed: John C. McLemore (Seal) by his attorney Thomas J. Anderson (Seal)

(Five-cent Jefferson revenue stamp affixed.)

State of Tennessee – Coffee County

Personally appeared before me, **Grantham Goodlaw, J.P.**, one of the acting Justices of the Peace for said county and state, the above-named **Thomas J. Anderson**, attorney-in-fact for **John**

C. McLemore, who acknowledged the execution of the foregoing instrument for the purposes therein contained.

Witness my hand on this 7th day of January A.D. 1860.

Grantham Goodlaw, J.P.

by **Jas. Harrison**, Clerk

Historical Note

This 1860 contract marks one of the earliest documented business transactions involving the Anderson family in Coffee County. It reveals not only John W. Anderson's role in local development but also the continued connection between **Sina Anderson's** lineage and the economic growth of Middle Tennessee on the eve of the Civil War.

Editor's Note:

Transcribed from the original document held within the Anderson family papers and reproduced here for historical *preservation in **The Sina Anderson Family Legacy** collection.*

Image Source:

Original Land Exchange Agreement between John W. Anderson of Coffee County, Tennessee, and John C. McLemore of San Francisco, California, dated January 5 and February 20, 1860.

Document includes original seals, signatures, and a five-cent Jefferson revenue stamp.

Preserved in the Anderson Family Archives and reproduced here courtesy of the family's private collection.

Archival Preservation Note:

The original 1860 *Memorandum of Agreement* remains in fragile yet legible condition, preserved within the Anderson Family Archives. The paper exhibits light fading and natural age toning, with handwritten ink still visible throughout. A digital enhancement of the document has been created to ensure its continued readability and historical integrity. Both original and enhanced versions are now stored in the family's digital preservation collection and secured archival binder.

This record stands as a tangible link to the business life of John W. Anderson and the enduring legacy of the Anderson family's stewardship of Tennessee lands.

Closing Reflection – The Ties That Endure

This document not only preserves the legal work of John W. Anderson but also deepens the understanding of the Anderson family's inner bonds.

It confirms that **Sina Anderson**, daughter of Captain John W. Anderson, later married **Joseph Good**, the brother of **Thomas A. Anderson**, who had served as attorney-in-fact in the very exchange recorded here. Through that marriage, the Anderson and Good families became forever intertwined — bound by faith, land, and enduring love.

The same signatures that once sealed an agreement of property now stand as symbols of unity within the family line. What began as a transaction of land became, in Spirit, a covenant of heritage — linking generations through both paper and purpose. Sina and Joseph carried that legacy forward, their lives completing what this document began: the merging of two steadfast families whose stories would continue to shape Coffee County and beyond.

Thus, the ink of 1860 still speaks — not only of land and law, but of kinship and Light that endures through every generation.

Narrative Lineage – The Anderson–Good Connection

The Anderson story begins with **Peter Anderson**, a man of faith and endurance who settled early in Middle Tennessee. From his strength came **Captain John W. Anderson**, a landholder and pillar of the community whose courage and fairness shaped the family's legacy along Bark Camp Fork and Mingo Creek.

Among Captain Anderson's children was **Sina Anderson**, whose life would unite two strong family lines. She **first married Joseph Anderson**, a union that carried forward the bloodline and spirit of her father's house. After Joseph's passing, she **later married Edward Good**, thereby weaving the Anderson and Good families into one enduring branch.

Through these unions, Sina became both bridge and matriarch—linking kin by faith, love, and steadfastness on the same Tennessee soil her father had once claimed and defended. Her sons, **Joseph Anderson, Jr., Thomas A. Anderson, and Outlaw V. Anderson**, carried those values forward, each reflecting the same quiet strength and integrity that had long defined their line.

Across time, the names changed, but the Light did not. From Peter's frontier courage to Captain John W.'s integrity, from Sina's grace to the generations that followed, the Anderson–Good family stands as a testament to heritage preserved through love, faith, and remembrance.

Their story is not simply written in deeds and records, but in the enduring bond of family — a light that still shines through every descendant who remembers.

Peter Anderson

|
└──Captain John W. Anderson

　　|
　　└──Sina Anderson (Anderson Good)

　　　　├──First husband: Joseph Anderson

　　　　│　├──Joseph Anderson Jr.

　　　　│　├──Thomas A. Anderson

　　　　│　└──Outlaw V. Anderson

　　　　|

　　　　└──Later husband: Edward Good

Family Line Summary

The Anderson–Good family line stands as one of faith, endurance, and unity. From **Peter Anderson's** early frontier days through **Captain John W. Anderson's** steadfast leadership, each generation built upon the courage and integrity of the one before.

When **Sina Anderson** came of age, she carried forward not only her father's legacy but the strength of an entire lineage. Through her marriage to **Joseph Anderson** and later **Edward Good**, she joined two enduring Tennessee families whose roots and faith were deeply intertwined.

Her sons — **Joseph Anderson Jr., Thomas A. Anderson, and Outlaw V. Anderson** — carried forward the Anderson name and values into a new generation, extending the family's presence across the growing American frontier. Each of them reflected a different facet of the family spirit: leadership, resilience, and quiet devotion.

The bonds formed through Sina's life joined the Anderson and Good families in both heritage and heart. What began in the hills and valleys of Coffee County became more than a record of names — it became a living testament to perseverance, love, and the Light that connects generations.

Through the lives of those who came before, the family's strength endures. Through remembrance, their Light continues to shine.

Historical Note – Edward Good

Edward Good became part of the Anderson story through his marriage to **Sina Anderson** after the passing of her first husband, **Joseph Anderson**, who was the brother of **Thomas A. Anderson**. Through these connections, Sina's life wove together two respected Tennessee families—the Andersons and the Goods—each known for their faith, perseverance, and devotion to family.

Edward was a man of quiet strength and enduring kindness. His life reflected the steadfast spirit of those who worked in the Tennessee land—rooted in honesty, guided by faith, and committed to those he loved. When he and Sina married, their union brought comfort, stability, and a sense of renewal after years of loss and transition.

Together, they upheld the family's values of integrity and compassion, ensuring that the generations to come would inherit not only the Anderson name, but also the heart and endurance of the Good family line. Their home became a gathering place of peace and remembrance—a living bridge between past and future.

Through Edward's steadfast presence and Sina's enduring grace, the two families became one—joined not only by marriage, but by purpose, legacy, and Light that still shines through their descendants today.

Reflection – The Union of Peace

In the joining of the Anderson and Good families, a circle of Light was completed. What began in courage through Peter and Captain John W. Anderson found its peace in Sina's faith and Edward's steadfast heart. Together they built more than a home — they created harmony between two lineages whose roots run deep in the Tennessee hills.

Through their patience and love, the Anderson-Good legacy was renewed. Their union reminds us that healing often comes not through grand moments, but through simple acts of kindness, shared prayers, and the quiet strength to begin again.

Affirmation – The Line Restored in Light:
"I honor the bonds that unite the Anderson and Good families. Through love, understanding, and divine guidance, their hearts became one.
May the Light that joined them continue to guide their descendants,
bringing peace to the past, purpose to the present, and blessing to the generations yet to come."

— *End of the Sina Anderson Line* —

Coffee County, Tennessee · Circa 1860–1900

"Through remembrance, the roots endure."

The Legacy of Sina Anderson (Anderson Good)

Daughter of Captain John W. Anderson – Keeper of Faith and Family Light

Introduction:

Born into the

Anderson line of Coffee County, Tennessee, **Sina Anderson** carried forward the courage, grace, and devotion that defined her family. Her life bridged generations, uniting strength, and compassion through her marriages to **Joseph Anderson** and later **Edward Good**.

Through these unions, two respected families became one enduring heritage — the Andersons and the Goods — joined by faith, perseverance, and love of home. Sina's story stands as both a continuation and a healing of lines: where the labor of her forebears met the peace of her own heart.

In her life, the Light of the Anderson legacy found its reflection in the Good family's enduring kindness — and through them, the seed of remembrance continues to grow.

— *The Daughter Who United Two Lines* —

Faith · Heritage · Endurance

Sina Anderson (Anderson Good)

Born: March 25, 1835 – Jackson County, Alabama

Died: January 17, 1914 – Roff Town, Pontotoc County, Oklahoma, USA

Relation: 2nd Great-Grandaunt

Daughter of Captain John W. Anderson, Sina carried the family legacy westward through faith, endurance, and devotion. Her life bridged the Anderson and Good families, uniting two lines whose strength and compassion still echo through their descendants today.

Joseph Anderson

Born: March 25, 1835 – Hackberry Bottoms, Roane County, Tennessee

Died: May 7, 1872 – Tullahoma, Coffee County, Tennessee,

USA

Relation: Husband of Sina Anderson (Anderson Good)

Brother of Thomas A. Anderson and son of the extended Anderson line of Tennessee. Joseph's life reflected the same steadfastness and integrity that marked the family's legacy. He shared in the pioneering spirit of his generation — a man of faith, labor, and devotion. Through his marriage to Sina, the Anderson name continued in strength and unity, rooted in the Tennessee homeland they both loved.

Joseph J. Anderson

Born: March 30, 1863 – Forsyth, Monroe County, Georgia, USA

Died: June 25, 1945 – Pontotoc County, Oklahoma, USA

Relation: Son of Joseph Anderson and Sina Anderson (Anderson Good)

Joseph J. Anderson carried the family legacy from the Tennessee homeland into the growing frontier of Oklahoma.

A man of perseverance and faith, he represented the next generation of Anderson strength — bridging the post-Civil War South to a new century of change. His life stands as a testament to endurance, family devotion, and the quiet courage that has

Joseph Anderson Jr.

John Watson Anderson

Born: September 21, 1865 – Monroe County, Georgia, USA

Died: May 25, 1897 – Roff, Pontotoc County, Oklahoma, USA

Relation: Son of Joseph Anderson and Sina Anderson (Anderson Good)

John Watson Anderson lived during a time of movement and renewal in the post-Civil War South. He followed his family westward from Georgia into the open lands of Oklahoma, carrying with him the faith and determination of his Anderson heritage. Though his life was brief, his journey symbolized the courage of those who sought new beginnings while holding fast to family and faith. His name endures as a link between the Tennessee roots and the Oklahoma frontier that shaped later generations.

always defined the Anderson line

.

John W. Anderson

Thomas Augley Anderson

Born: January 18, 1867 – Hillsboro, Coffee County, Tennessee, USA

Died: 1950 – Pontotoc County, Oklahoma, USA

Relation: Son of Joseph Anderson and Sina Anderson (Anderson Good)

Thomas Augley Anderson was born in the rolling hills of Coffee County, Tennessee, a region shaped by the strength and resilience of the Anderson family. As a young man, he followed the family migration westward, eventually settling in Oklahoma, where faith and hard work guided his life. His story reflects the enduring spirit of the Anderson line — rooted in Tennessee soil, yet always seeking new ground where family, perseverance, and Light could take root once more.

]

Thomas A. Anderson

Outlaw Vicalpine Anderson

Born: October 17, 1871 – Hillsboro, Coffee County, Tennessee, USA

Died: March 9, 1943 – Plainview, Hale County, Texas, USA

Relation: Son of Joseph Anderson and Sina Anderson (Anderson Good)

Born during the family's final years in Tennessee, Outlaw Vicalpine Anderson carried the Anderson legacy beyond state lines and into the wide plains of Texas. His life embodied the pioneer's courage — moving west in search of opportunity while upholding the family's enduring faith and work ethic. Through his journey, the Anderson line extended into a new frontier, linking the hills of Tennessee and the red soil of Oklahoma to the open fields of Texas. His path completed the migration that began generations before, sealing the family's story as one of endurance, movement, and Light across the American heartland.

Outlaw Vicalpine Anderson

The Children of Sina Anderson (Anderson Good)

From the quiet hills of Tennessee to the plains of Oklahoma and Texas, the sons of **Sina and Joseph Anderson** carried the family name into a new century. **Joseph J., John Watson, Thomas Augley,** and **Outlaw Vicalpine Anderson** each lived in their own way the values that had defined the Anderson line for generations — faith, resilience, and devotion to family.

Their journeys tell the story of a people who refused to let distance or hardship sever the bonds of kinship. Through their work, their homes, and their children, the Light of the Anderson heritage continued to grow, branching ever outward yet remaining rooted in the strength of those who came before.

From Tennessee soil to Oklahoma fields and Texas plains, the sons of Sina carried the name, the faith, and the heart of their mother's legacy. Theirs was a generation of movement and endurance — and through them, the Anderson spirit lives on in every descendant who remembers their name.

Sina's second Husband:

John Edward Good Sr.

Born: 1810 – North Carolina, USA

Died: 1880 – Roff Town, Pontotoc County, Oklahoma, USA

Relation: Father of Edward Good (the second husband of Sina Anderson [Anderson Good])

John Edward Good Sr. was a pioneer of quiet dignity and enduring faith. Born in the early years of the nineteenth century, his life bridged the rugged lands of North Carolina and the open territories of Oklahoma. He guided his family through seasons of change with patience, integrity, and an unwavering belief in hard work and devotion to home. Through his son Edward Good's marriage to Sina Anderson, the Good family became woven into the Anderson heritage — a union that joined two lines of strength, service, and Light across generations.

Delila A. Ellison Good

Born: 1823 – Tennessee, USA

Died: 1880 – Hillsboro, Coffee County, Tennessee, USA

Relation: First wife of John Edward Good Sr.; Mother of Edward Good (the second husband of Sina Anderson [Anderson Good])

Delila A. Ellison Good was a woman of faith and endurance, whose quiet devotion shaped the early Good family line. Born in the hills of Tennessee, she lived a life rooted in family and guided by steadfast belief. Her marriage to John Edward Good Sr. brought forth a lineage of integrity and perseverance that would later join with the Andersons through her son Edward Good. Though her years ended in Hillsboro, the strength of her spirit continued westward through her children, uniting two families in purpose and Light.

Children: 1st married:

Griffin M. Good

Born: 1844 – Tennessee, USA

Died: November 10, 1863 – Chicago, Cook County, Illinois, USA

Relation: Son of John Edward Good Sr. and Delila A. Ellison Good; Brother of Edward Good

Griffin M. Good lived during one of the most turbulent chapters in American history. Born in Tennessee, he came of age as the nation divided, and his path led him far from home into the trials of the Civil War. Passing away in 1863 in Chicago, his life was brief yet marked by courage and duty. Through his sacrifice, the Good family's legacy of service was forever written into the story of the Anderson–Good line. Though his years were few, his name stands among those who gave their lives in the hope of peace and unity for generations to come.

Sarah Jane Good

Born: February 27, 1848 – Wilson County, Tennessee, USA

Died: May 20, 1903 – Marshall County, Oklahoma, USA

Relation: Daughter of John Edward Good Sr. and Delila A. Ellison Good; Stepdaughter of Sina Anderson (Anderson Good)

Sarah Jane Good grew up amid the hills of Tennessee and journeyed west as the frontier opened. Through faith and perseverance, she carried forward the Good family's quiet strength into the lands that would become Oklahoma. Her life bridged two families and two eras — the Tennessee homeland of her birth and the new frontier of her later years. As the stepdaughter of Sina Anderson (Anderson Good), she became part of the enduring union between the Good and Anderson lines, her story joining the broader heritage of courage, endurance, and Light that defines their shared legacy.

Thomas Bailey Good

Born: February 1850 – Wilson County, Tennessee, USA

Died: Before 1930 – Coffee County, Tennessee, USA

Relation: Son of John Edward Good Sr. and Delila A. Ellison Good; Stepson of Sina Anderson (Anderson Good)

Thomas Bailey Good was born amid the farmlands of Wilson County, Tennessee, and spent much of his life near the family's ancestral roots in Coffee County. A man of quiet diligence, he carried forward the work and values instilled by his parents, John Edward Good Sr., and Delila Ellison Good. Through his stepmother, Sina Anderson (Anderson Good), his life became interwoven with the Anderson line, joining two families whose histories shaped the heart of early Tennessee. His story stands as a reminder of steadfast faith, humble labor, and the enduring ties of family that stretch across generations.

John Edward Good Jr.

Born: March 21, 1852 – Franklin County, Tennessee, USA

Died: March 5, 1931 – Roff, Pontotoc County, Oklahoma, USA

Relation: Son of John Edward Good Sr. and Delila A. Ellison Good; Stepson of Sina Anderson (Anderson Good)

John Edward Good Jr. was part of the generation that carried the Good family westward from the hills of Tennessee into the open plains of Oklahoma. Born in Franklin County, he grew up with the strong values of faith and perseverance that marked the Good name. His later years in Roff, Pontotoc County — the same community where Sina Anderson (Anderson Good) would one day rest — reflected the quiet continuation of family bonds through time and distance. Through his life, the Good legacy remained rooted in service, faith, and devotion, joining harmoniously with the Anderson line to form one enduring heritage of Light and remembrance.

Martha Louisa "Mattie" Good

Born: February 15, 1854 – Franklin County, Tennessee, USA
Died: June 16, 1897 – Coffee County, Tennessee, USA

Relation: Daughter of John Edward Good Sr. and Delila A. Ellison Good; Stepdaughter of Sina Anderson (Anderson Good)

Martha Louisa "Mattie" Good was born in the heart of Tennessee, where the Good and Anderson families' stories intertwined. Known for her warmth and gentle spirit, she embodied the quiet strength of her lineage. Though her life was brief, her years were filled with faith, family, and devotion to the land she called home. Her passing in Coffee County closed a chapter of the early Good family's Tennessee years — a chapter remembered through love, legacy, and the unbroken bond between two families joined by Light.

Nancy Good

Born: About 1856 – Franklin County, Tennessee, USA
Died: Before 1870
Relation: Daughter of John Edward Good Sr. and Delila A. Ellison Good; Stepdaughter of Sina Anderson (Anderson Good)

Nancy Good lived only a brief time, but her name remains a gentle part of the Good family story. Born during the family's years in Franklin County, Tennessee, she was one of the youngest children of John Edward and Delila Ellison Good. Though her life ended before the family's later move west, her memory lives through her siblings who carried the Good legacy into Oklahoma and beyond. In remembrance, she stands as one of the many early lights in a lineage built upon love, faith, and the eternal bond of family.

Robert Edward Good

Born: May 1859 – Elk River, Franklin County, Tennessee, USA

Died: 1954 – Hobart, Kiowa County, Oklahoma, USA

Relation: Son of John Edward Good Sr. and Delila A. Ellison Good; Brother of Edward Good (the second husband of Sina Anderson [Anderson Good])

Robert Edward Good was born along the Elk River in Franklin County, Tennessee, during the final years of his family's life in the South. A man of quiet faith and resolve, he journeyed west as part of the generation that helped settle the Oklahoma territories. Through his life's work and steady character, he carried forward the spirit of his parents, John Edward, and Delila Good. His long life spanned a century of change, and through it all he upheld the family's devotion to honesty, service, and kinship. His presence in Oklahoma linked the past and future of the Good lineage, ensuring that the Light of his

Introduction to the Anderson Line of Joseph Anderson

The Anderson line that Joseph was born into was part of the early wave of Tennessee settler families known for education, land ownership, and strong community presence. These were not drifting pioneers but rooted builders, men and women who believed in establishing homes, improving the land, and creating stability for their children. Joseph inherited this legacy of resilience and purpose. His people came from the Tennessee river valleys and foothill regions—Roane County, Monroe County, and later Coffee County, forming a network of Anderson relatives who worked the soil, held property, served local affairs, and endured the upheavals of the Civil War.

Joseph's ancestry represents one branch of a much larger line, shaped by the same values that would carry his own children westward into Oklahoma and Texas. What follows is the lineage as far back as can be determined, showing the roots from which Joseph—and Sina's entire family legacy—emerged.

☆ Thomas Von Albade Anderson

(1802–1893)

Born: 15 May 1802 • Jefferson County, Tennessee

Died: 28 Feb 1893 • Tullahoma, Coffee County, Tennessee

This is exactly the kind of solid ancestral detail your Legacy books are built on.

Now I can write the **full generational entry** for him — matching the tone and style of your other Legacy series volumes.

Below is a polished section you can paste directly into the book.

⭐ Father of Joseph Anderson

Thomas Von Albade Anderson (1802–1893)

Thomas Von Albade Anderson was born on May 15, 1802, in Jefferson County, Tennessee, a region that was part of the earliest push westward during the post-Revolution settlement of the state. His life spanned the entire 19th century, reaching from the era of frontier cabins and hand-cut roads all the way into the age of railroads, telegraphs, and the early modern South. Few people of his time lived long enough to witness such sweeping change.

Thomas settled in Coffee County, Tennessee, becoming part of the growing community around Tullahoma. His long life and consistent presence in the county helped anchor the extended Anderson family as they transitioned from their early footholds in East Tennessee toward the middle portion of the state. He is recorded as a landholder, a farmer, and one of the older patriarchs of the Anderson line whose descendants would later spread across Tennessee, Oklahoma, and Texas.

Thomas lived to the remarkable age of ninety-one years, passing on February 28, 1893, in Tullahoma. His longevity made him a witness to multiple generations—he lived long enough to see Joseph grow, marry Sina, raise their children, and for the Anderson line to expand westward once again. His influence is felt in the values of education, land care, and resilience that remained strong in his descendants.

Thomas Von Albade Anderson represents the **first firmly documented generation above Joseph**, the root from which the Coffee County Andersons emerged and carried their lineage forward into new frontiers.

☆ Mother of Joseph Anderson

Hannah Barclay Moore (1807–1867)

Born: 1807 • Dandridge, Jefferson County, Tennessee

Died: 1867 • Tullahoma, Coffee County, Tennessee

Hannah Barclay Moore was born in 1807 in Dandridge, Jefferson County, Tennessee—one of the oldest towns in the state and a hub for early Scottish Irish settlers. Her childhood would have been shaped by the culture of frontier families who valued faith, education, and close-knit community life. Hannah's Moore family belonged to a long-standing group of Jefferson County residents, many of whom had migrated there before 1800 and established strong ties with the surrounding counties of East Tennessee.

Hannah married **Thomas Von Albade Anderson**, uniting two early Tennessee lines. Together they raised their children during a time when the state was shifting from frontier homesteads into organized counties, schools, and small towns. By the time the Anderson family moved toward Coffee County, Hannah had already become one of the stabilizing influences of the household, helping establish the values and structure their children would carry into adulthood.

Her life, like many women of her time, was marked by strength, longevity, and quiet leadership. She lived long enough to see Tennessee transformed through settlement, statehood, and the early rise of the railroad systems. Hannah passed away in 1867 in Tullahoma, Coffee County—just five years before her son Joseph's death and six years before the birth of her grandson **Outlaw Vicalpine Anderson.**

Though her name appears in records less often than the men of her generation, the legacy she left through her children and grandchildren is unmistakable. The Anderson values of perseverance, literacy, and resilience can be traced directly to her influence.

She stands as the maternal pillar of Joseph Anderson's lineage.

⭐ Children of Thomas Von Albade Anderson & Hannah Barclay Moore

(Beginning the full sibling list — we will add each one you send)

1. Von Albade Anderson

Birth: April 8, 1827, • Soldiers Rest, Jefferson County, Tennessee

Death: March 7, 1896, • Knox County, Tennessee

Von Albade Anderson was the eldest documented child of Thomas and Hannah. Born in Jefferson County before the family moved toward the middle part of the state, he represents the continuation of the family's early East Tennessee roots. He lived through the Civil War era, Reconstruction, and the growth of Tennessee's post-war communities. His later life in Knox County connects the Anderson family back into the

Knoxville region, showing how wide the Anderson descendants eventually spread.

☆ 2. Amanda Frances Anderson

Birth: 1828 • Tennessee, USA

Death: Coffee County, Tennessee

Amanda Frances Anderson was one of the early daughters of Thomas and Hannah. Born during the family's years in East Tennessee, she came of age as the Andersons began moving toward the middle part of the state. Her life in Coffee County places her directly within the heart of the Anderson family's growing presence around Tullahoma.

Though records from her era are limited, Amanda represents the strong line of Anderson women who helped establish households, support extended kin, and anchor the family during decades of change. Her life in Coffee County ties her permanently to the region her parents would later call home.

⭐ 3. Laura Jane Augusta Anderson

Birth: June 3, 1829, • Roane County, Tennessee

Death: January 24, 1900, • Nashville, Davidson County, Tennessee

Laura Jane Augusta Anderson was born in Roane County during the family's transitional years between East and Middle Tennessee. Her birth marks the Anderson family's presence along the Tennessee River valleys before their eventual move into Coffee County.

Laura later made her home in Nashville, placing her among the first Andersons of her generation to live in an urban, rapidly growing Tennessee city. Her life bridged two worlds — the rural origins of her parents and the increasingly modern environment of the state's capital. Laura's long life reflects the Anderson tradition of education, endurance, and adaptability across changing times.

⭐ 4. Franklin Joseph Anderson

Birth: 1831 • Jefferson County, Tennessee

Death: December 29, 1861, • Laurel, Jones County, Mississippi

Franklin Joseph Anderson was born in 1831 during the final years the Anderson family lived in Jefferson County. He represents the generation of young Tennessee men whose lives were shaped by the growing tensions that would soon erupt into the Civil War.

Franklin's death in Laurel, Mississippi, in late 1861 places him among the earliest losses of that conflict. Whether serving in a Tennessee regiment or among the many volunteers who joined from surrounding states, Franklin became part of the great upheaval that marked his era.

His early passing left no long record, yet his life is woven into the story of the Andersons who sacrificed, migrated, and endured through one of the most defining times in American history.

5. Cassandra Moore Anderson

Birth: January 12, 1833, • Athens, McMinn County, Tennessee

Death: February 9, 1833, • Athens, McMinn County, Tennessee

Cassandra Moore Anderson was born in early 1833 during the Anderson family's brief time in Athens, Tennessee. Her life was only a few weeks long, a tender moment in the family's history marked by both joy and deep sorrow.

Though her time on earth was short, Cassandra's place in the Anderson lineage remains important. She represents the many children of early Tennessee families whose brief lives shaped the strength, compassion, and resilience of their parents.

Her memory stands with the other Anderson children as part of the story of a family that endured loss while continuing to build a future across Tennessee and, eventually, the West.

6. Victoria Cassandra Anderson

Birth: August 25, 1834, • Hackberry Bottoms, Roane County, Tennessee

Death: March 24, 1901

Victoria Cassandra Anderson was born in Hackberry Bottoms during the Anderson family's move through Roane County. Her name reflects a family tradition of remembrance — she was given "Cassandra" to honor her infant sister who passed the previous year.

Victoria lived a long life and represents the strength and resilience of the Anderson women of her generation. She experienced Tennessee's shifting landscapes — from frontier communities and early farms to the more established towns that developed after the Civil War.

Her presence in the records and her long lifespan anchor her firmly within the broader Anderson story, bridging the early Tennessee settlements with the new century that followed.

⭐ 7. Joseph Anderson

Birth: March 25, 1835, • Hackberry Bottoms, Roane County, Tennessee

Death: May 7, 1872, • Tullahoma, Coffee County, Tennessee

Joseph Anderson was born in Hackberry Bottoms during the family's final years in Roane County. He represents the pivotal generation that carried the Anderson line from East Tennessee into the heart of Coffee County, where their roots would deepen for decades to come.

Joseph married **Sina Anderson (Good)** and together they became the parents of four sons—Joseph J. Anderson Jr., John Watson Anderson, Thomas Aughley Anderson, and Outlaw Vicalpine Anderson. Through these sons, the Anderson line expanded westward into Oklahoma and Texas, forming the foundation of the modern branches of the family.

Joseph's life was marked by hard work, deep family ties, and a quiet strength that defined his generation. His early death in 1872 left Sina a widow with young children, yet the values he passed on continued through every descendant who carried the Anderson name. He stands as the central figure of this branch, the link between the early Tennessee pioneers and the generations who would build new lives in the West.

☆ 8. Hannah Minerva Anderson

Birth: January 25, 1838, • Blue Cliffs, Roane County, Tennessee

Death: July 20, 1895, • Tullahoma, Coffee County, Tennessee

Hannah Minerva Anderson was born in the Blue Cliffs area of Roane County, a region known for its ridgelines, river valleys, and early frontier settlements. She represents the final group of Anderson children born before the family's permanent move into Coffee County.

Her life carried her from the river country of Roane County into the developing crossroads town of Tullahoma, where she lived through the Civil War, Reconstruction, and the transformation of the region through railroads and industry.

Hannah remained close to her extended family and lived out her years in Coffee County, anchoring the Anderson presence there alongside her siblings. Her long life reflects the endurance, adaptability, and stability that characterized the Anderson women of her generation.

Through her story, we see the continuation of the family's steady movement westward within Tennessee, setting the stage for the later migration of her nephews into Oklahoma and Texas.

9. William Moore Anderson

Birth: March 15, 1840, • Jefferson County, Tennessee

Death: May 5, 1905, • Tullahoma, Coffee County, Tennessee

William Moore Anderson was born in Jefferson County during the final years of the Anderson family's time in East Tennessee. His middle name, *Moore*, honors his mother's lineage — a tradition often found in 19th-century families who wished to preserve both the paternal and maternal lines.

William grew up during the family's transition from the river valleys of Jefferson and Roane Counties to the rolling lands of Coffee County. His adult life unfolded in Tullahoma, where he witnessed the turmoil of the Civil War, the rebuilding of the town afterward, and the rise of the railroad that would redefine the region.

He remained close to his siblings and extended kin, becoming one of the anchors of the Coffee County Andersons. His long life — spanning 65 years — reflects the endurance and consistency that marked the Anderson men of his generation. William's presence in the family's Tennessee chapters shows how deeply rooted the Andersons became in Tullahoma before the next generations pushed further west into Oklahoma and Texas.

10. Outlaw Vic Alpin Anderson

Birth: May 4, 1845, • Jefferson County, Tennessee

Death: October 7, 1922, • Henryetta, Okmulgee County, Oklahoma

Outlaw Vic Alpin Anderson was born in Jefferson County during the final period before the Anderson family made their long, steady move westward across Tennessee. His striking name — *Outlaw Vic Alpin* — reflects a powerful family naming tradition that would later appear again in his nephew, **Outlaw Vicalpine Anderson**, showing a deep continuity within the line. Outlaw grew to adulthood in Tennessee but eventually joined the western movement that carried so many Anderson descendants into Oklahoma. By the time of his death in 1922 at Henryetta, Okmulgee County, he had become part of the expanding Anderson presence that helped shape early Oklahoma communities.

He represents the bridge generation between the old Tennessee settlements and the new frontier families who established permanent roots in the West. Outlaw's long life, spanning seventy-seven years, carried him from antebellum Tennessee through the Civil War, Reconstruction, Oklahoma Territory days, and into the early years of Oklahoma statehood.

His story embodies the pioneering spirit of the Andersons and stands as a testament to the endurance and westward vision of his family.

☆ 11. Thomas Alexander Anderson

Birth: October 25, 1847, • Jefferson County, Tennessee
Death: March 5, 1855, • Coffee County, Tennessee

Thomas Alexander Anderson was born in Jefferson County near the end of the Anderson family's time in East Tennessee. He was one of the younger children of Thomas Von Albade Anderson and Hannah Barclay Moore, arriving during a period of constant movement as the family transitioned toward Coffee County.

His childhood was brief. Thomas passed away in 1855 in Coffee County at only seven years old, leaving behind a tender place in the family's story. Like many children of the era, his short life reflects the challenges families faced before modern medical care, particularly during times of relocation and frontier hardship.

Though his time was short, Thomas Alexander remains an important part of the Anderson lineage, representing the younger generation whose memory continued through the children and grandchildren of his surviving siblings.

 Father of Thomas Von Albade Anderson

Joseph Inslee Anderson (1757–1837)

Birth: November 5, 1757, • White Marsh, Philadelphia County, Pennsylvania

Death: April 17, 1837, • Washington City, District of Columbia

Joseph Inslee Anderson was born in 1757 in White Marsh, Pennsylvania, during the final decades of the colonial period. He came of age as the American Revolution unfolded, and his life would mirror the rise of the new nation itself. He served as an officer in the Revolutionary War, participating in several major battles, and was part of the generation of young men whose service would shape the birth of the United States.

After the war, Joseph moved southward into the developing frontier settlements that would become Tennessee. His intelligence, leadership, and military background positioned him as a respected figure in unfamiliar territory. He went on to become a distinguished statesperson, serving as a **United States Senator from Tennessee** and later as the **Comptroller of the U.S. Treasury** under multiple presidents.

Joseph spent his final years in Washington, D.C., where he continued public service until his death in 1837. His life represents one of the most significant American stories in your ancestry — a man who helped build the nation, establish

Tennessee's early political identity, and pass down a legacy of public service, education, and leadership to the Anderson generations that followed.

From the Revolutionary battlefield to the halls of the Senate, Joseph Inslee Anderson stands as one of the most historically important ancestors in the Anderson Family Legacy.

☆ Mother of Thomas Von Albade Anderson

Patience Outlaw (1777–1864)

Birth: March 1, 1777, • Duplin County, North Carolina

Death: September 17, 1864, • Coffee County, Tennessee

Patience Outlaw was born in 1777 in Duplin County, North Carolina, into one of the old southern families whose roots reached back to the colonial frontier. Her family name — *Outlaw* — is one of the most recognizable and enduring surnames in early Carolina and Tennessee history, and it would become a treasured name carried forward through multiple Anderson generations.

She married **Joseph Inslee Anderson**, Revolutionary War officer, early Tennessee statesperson, and future United States Senator. Patience became the quiet center of this distinguished household, raising children during the turbulent years when Tennessee transformed from a wilderness territory into an organized state.

Patience's life spanned an extraordinary period of American history. Born in the last decades of the colonial world, she lived through the Revolution, the founding of the nation, the War of 1812, westward expansion, and even the beginning of the Civil War. By the time she died in Coffee County in 1864, she had seen ninety years of national transformation.

Her move from North Carolina to Tennessee followed the broader southern migration that shaped the early frontier. Her later years in Coffee County placed her close to several of her children and grandchildren, including the branch that would lead to **Joseph Anderson (1835–1872)** and the family's westward expansion into Oklahoma and Texas.

Patience's legacy is woven directly into the Anderson family identity — her strength, longevity, and heritage echo through every generation that carries the *Outlaw* name forward.

☆ Children of Joseph Inslee Anderson & Patience Outlaw

(Beginning the full sibling list — we will add each one you send)

---

1. William Anderson

Birth: 1794 • Washington City, District of Columbia

Death: August 27, 1881, • Washington City, District of Columbia

William Anderson was one of the eldest documented children of Joseph Inslee Anderson and Patience Outlaw. Born in the nation's capital while his father served in the early federal government, William's birthplace reflects the Anderson family's close involvement in the formation of the United States.

He lived an exceptionally long life for his era, remaining in Washington City until his death in 1881 at the age of eighty-seven. His lifetime spanned from the early republic to Reconstruction, making him a witness to the first century of American history.

His presence in Washington suggests a continuation of the family's connection to public service, law, or administrative work. William stands as a reminder that the Anderson family's influence extended far beyond Tennessee — rooted in both the southern frontier and the halls of the early federal government.

 2. Alexander Outlaw Anderson

Birth: November 10, 1794, • Soldiers Rest, Knox County, Tennessee

Death: May 23, 1869, • Knoxville, Knox County, Tennessee

Alexander Outlaw Anderson was born in Soldiers Rest, Knox County, during the early years when Tennessee was transitioning from frontier territory into a developing state. His middle name, *Outlaw*, honored his mother's powerful Carolina lineage — a family name that became a repeating heritage marker across multiple Anderson generations.

Alexander became one of the most prominent members of the Anderson family. He followed in the footsteps of his father, **Senator Joseph Inslee Anderson**, and pursued a career in public life. He served in the **United States Senate**, representing Tennessee, and was deeply involved in law, government, and the political shaping of the state. His public service placed the

Anderson family at the heart of Tennessee's early political identity.

Throughout his life, Alexander remained centered in Knoxville, a vital political and cultural hub of early Tennessee. His lengthy career, which extended through the antebellum era, the rise of sectional tensions, and the beginning of Reconstruction, reflects the profound influence of the Anderson name in regional and national affairs.

Alexander Outlaw Anderson stands as one of the most historically significant figures in this generation — a statesperson, a bearer of the Outlaw lineage, and a critical link between the Revolutionary generation and the later movement of the family into Coffee County and beyond.

☆ 3. Thomas Von Albade Anderson

Birth: May 15, 1802, • Jefferson County, Tennessee

Death: February 28, 1893, • Tullahoma, Coffee County, Tennessee

Thomas Von Albade Anderson was born in Jefferson County during the years when Tennessee was still a young, developing state. He represents the bridge between the prominent public life of his father, **Senator Joseph Inslee Anderson**, and the steady, community-rooted life that his own children and grandchildren would build across Tennessee and the American frontier.

Unlike his brothers who remained connected to Washington or Knoxville political circles, Thomas followed the westward movement that carried families from East Tennessee into the fertile lands of Coffee County. His long life — ninety-one years — made him a witness to the entire 19th century: from the frontier era, through the Civil War, and into Reconstruction.

It was Thomas who became the patriarchal root of the Coffee County Andersons. Through his marriage to **Hannah Barclay Moore**, he fathered a large family of eleven children, including **Joseph Anderson (1835–1872)** — the ancestor through whom your line continues.

His descendants carried the family into Oklahoma and Texas, extending the Anderson legacy far beyond Tennessee.

Thomas Von Albade Anderson stands as the foundational figure of your branch of the Anderson line: a man who preserved the family's values of resilience, literacy, and land stewardship and passed them forward into the generations that followed.

☆ 4. Pierce Butler Anderson

Birth: 1806 • McMinn County, Tennessee

Death: October 3, 1861, • Lewisburg, Logan County, Kentucky

Pierce Butler Anderson was born in 1806 during the Anderson family's years in McMinn County. His name reflects a cultural pattern of the time — many families name children after states people, military figures, or respected public leaders. "Pierce Butler" was a well-known Revolutionary figure and U.S. Senator, indicating that the Anderson family remained closely aligned with political and civic ideals.

Pierce's adult life carried him northward into Kentucky, where he lived during a period of rising national tension. His 1861 death in Lewisburg came at the very beginning of the Civil War, marking him among the many southern families touched early by the conflict. While details of his service or circumstances remain limited, his death in the first year of the war places him in the generation that bridged the world of early Tennessee statehood with the turmoil of national division.

Pierce Butler Anderson represents the branch of the Anderson family that extended beyond Tennessee into Kentucky, adding another geographic thread to a family already spread across Washington City, Knoxville, Coffee County, and later Oklahoma and Texas.

His legacy remains part of the broader Anderson story — a family rooted in public service, resilience, and the steady westward expansion that defined the American frontier.

⭐ 5. Addison A. Anderson

Birth: 1807 • McMinn County, Tennessee

Death: 1883 • St. Louis, St. Louis County, Missouri

Addison A. Anderson was born in 1807 during the Anderson family's years in McMinn County, Tennessee. He belonged to the generation that grew up during the formative decades of Tennessee statehood — a period defined by expansion, settlement, and shifting political identity as the new nation found its footing.

Addison's life carried him far beyond Tennessee. He moved west into Missouri, eventually settling in St. Louis, a major commercial and cultural center of the 19th century. St. Louis was a crossroads of American migration — the "Gateway to the West" — and Addison's presence there reflects the Anderson family's early role in the nation's westward movement.

His long life, extending into the 1880s, placed him in the thick of tremendous national change: the westward expansion, the rise of the Mississippi River economy, the turmoil of the Civil War, and the industrial development that followed. Addison represents the branch of the Anderson family that migrated into the Midwest, adding yet another direction to the family's geographic spread.

His life in St. Louis stands as a testament to the Anderson family tradition of resilience, adaptability, and seeking opportunity. Through him, the Anderson name became part of the early fabric of one of America's most important frontier cities.

☆ 6. George Washington Anderson

Birth: 1809 • Jefferson City, Jefferson County, Tennessee
Death: 1832

George Washington Anderson was born in 1809 in Jefferson City, during the years when his father, **Senator Joseph Inslee Anderson**, remained deeply involved in Tennessee's early civic and political development. His given name — *George*

Washington — reflects the patriotic spirit of the era and the profound influence of America's Revolutionary generation on the Anderson household.

George's life was brief. He died in 1832, only in his early twenties, leaving behind few records and no known descendants. His early passing mirrors the pattern seen in many families of the frontier era, where illness, travel, and limited medical care often cut lives short.

☆ 7. James Madison Anderson

Birth: 1811 • Jonesboro, Jefferson County, Tennessee
Death: 1860 • Sacramento, Sacramento County, California

James Madison Anderson, born in 1811, carries a name that reflects the deep political atmosphere of his family. Named for *James Madison*, the fourth President of the United States, he was one of many Anderson children whose names honored America's founders and states people — a quiet reminder of the influence Joseph Inslee Anderson held as a Revolutionary War officer, U.S. Senator, and Comptroller of the Treasury.

James Madison Anderson represents one of the most dramatic geographic movements within this generation. While many of his siblings remained in Tennessee or moved into Kentucky and Missouri, James followed the great westward current of the mid-19th century all the way to California. His death in Sacramento in 1860 places him in the era of the California Gold Rush and the early settlement of the West Coast — a time when thousands traveled long distances in search of opportunity and prosperity.

Little is known about his life in California, but his presence there reflects the adventurous, pioneering spirit seen throughout the Anderson line. From Washington City to Knoxville, from Coffee County to the Midwest and the far West, the Anderson family spread across the early United States in extraordinary ways.

James Madison Anderson's journey adds a powerful thread to the family tapestry — showing that even from a deeply rooted Tennessee family, one son carried the Anderson legacy all the way to the Pacific frontier.

onward.

☆ 8. Margretta Anderson

Birth: Unknown

Death: October 21, 1857, • Jonesboro, Washington County, Tennessee

Margretta Anderson is one of the quieter branches of the Anderson family tree — a daughter whose life left few written records but whose presence completes the full circle of Joseph Inslee Anderson and Patience Outlaw's children. Her story reminds us that not every life is preserved in documents, yet each one shaped the family's heritage in its own way.

Born in the years when the Andersons lived in East Tennessee, Margretta grew up in a household shaped by political service, public duty, and strong family ties. While her brothers' movements carried them across Tennessee, Kentucky, Missouri, Oklahoma, and even to California, Margretta's life remained rooted closer to home.

Her death in 1857 in Jonesboro — one of the oldest towns in Tennessee and an early center of settlement and state politics — places her in the heart of the world her father helped build. Though we know little about her daily life, it is clear she belonged to the early Tennessee generation that carried the Anderson legacy forward during a time of rapid change and expansion.

Margretta represents the quieter side of the family story: the daughters whose experiences were seldom recorded but whose lives formed the foundation upon which future generations stood.

☆ William Anderson

Birth: 1723 • Trenton, Hunterdon County, New Jersey

Death: 1778 • Pennsylvania

William Anderson stands as the earliest firmly documented ancestor in your Anderson line — the patriarch whose life bridged the colonial era and the dawn of the American Revolution. Born in 1723 in Trenton, New Jersey, William lived during a time when the colonies were still under British rule, and the identity of "America" was only beginning to form.

By the 1770s, William Anderson was among the many men whose families found themselves caught in the upheaval leading to the Revolutionary War. He died in 1778, right in the midst of the conflict that would shape the future of the new nation. Though we do not yet know the exact circumstances of his passing, the timing places him directly within the turmoil, hardship, and sacrifice that marked the revolutionary period.

What makes William most significant in the family story is not only the era he lived in, but the legacy carried forward by his sons — especially **Joseph Inslee Anderson (1757–1837)**, the Revolutionary War officer, U.S. Senator, and Comptroller of the Treasury. William's values, resilience, and early American identity formed the foundation that his children carried into national service and into the building of Tennessee's early government.

Through William Anderson, the Anderson family story begins in the colonial Northeast and moves steadily south and west — eventually reaching East Tennessee, the frontier, Coffee County, and beyond.

His life marks the starting point of three centuries of Anderson history in America.

☆ Elizabeth Rosannah Inslee

Birth: 1728 • Newport, New Castle County, Delaware
Death: 1788 • Jonesboro, Washington County, Tennessee

Elizabeth Rosannah Inslee is one of the most important matriarchs in the Anderson family line — the woman whose lineage connects the colonial roots of Delaware and New Jersey to the early settling of Tennessee. Born in 1728 in Newport, Delaware, Elizabeth came from the Inslee family, an early American line known for literacy, civic involvement, and strong family ties.

Her marriage to **William Anderson (1723–1778)** united two prominent colonial families and produced several children, including **Joseph Inslee Anderson**, the Revolutionary War captain and later U.S. Senator from Tennessee. Through Elizabeth, the Inslee name became a lasting part of the Anderson identity, carried forward in the middle name of her son, and echoed through later generations.

Elizabeth's journey from the Mid-Atlantic to Tennessee reflects the broader movement of American families who left the older colonies in search of opportunity on the frontier. By the late 1780s, she was living in Jonesboro — one of the earliest established towns in Tennessee and the center of the short-lived **State of Franklin**, a bold early attempt at independence on the frontier. Her presence there places her at the heart of early Tennessee history during the years when the region was being shaped into the state it would become.

Her death in 1788, in Jonesboro, marks her as one of the earliest Anderson ancestors to enter Tennessee soil. Through Elizabeth Rosannah Inslee, the Anderson family inherits a heritage of early American settlement, frontier courage, and the strong family identity that carried the clan from the East Coast into the hills of Tennessee — and eventually into the generations that followed.

☆ Enoch Lucius Anderson

Birth: May 1, 1755, • Newport, New Castle County, Delaware

Death: April 21, 1824, • East Waterford, Juniata County, Pennsylvania

Enoch Lucius Anderson was born in 1755 in Newport, Delaware — the same community where his brother, **Joseph Inslee Anderson**, entered the world. Together they grew up in a family deeply rooted in the colonial Mid-Atlantic, during a time when tensions were rising between the American colonies and the British Crown.

Enoch's early years were shaped by the same patriotic spirit and civic duty that would later define his brother Joseph's public career. Though less is recorded about Enoch's personal achievements, his life reflects the path of many men of his generation: born in colonial America, shaped by the Revolution, and carried forward into the early decades of the new nation.

Unlike Joseph, who moved south into Tennessee and entered political life, Enoch remained in the region of Pennsylvania, one of the heartlands of early American settlement. His residence in East Waterford, Juniata County — an area of farms, mills, and early frontier communities — places him in the quiet but essential world of post-Revolution American life. Families like his formed the backbone of the young United States.

Enoch lived into 1824, long enough to see the country stabilize under Presidents Washington, Adams, Jefferson, and Madison, and into the expansion years that followed. His longevity places him firmly within the first generation of Americans to experience life before, during, and after the Revolution.

Though his descendants followed different paths than Joseph Inslee Anderson's prominent Tennessee line, Enoch Lucius Anderson represents a vital branch of the early Anderson family — carrying forward the same heritage of resilience, duty, and rooted American identity.

His life, recorded in both Delaware and Pennsylvania, firmly anchors the Anderson ancestry in the colonial era and shows how the family grew from shared origins into far-reaching American branches.

✹ Joseph Inslee Anderson

Birth: November 5, 1757, • White Marsh, Philadelphia County, Pennsylvania

Death: April 17, 1837, • Washington City, District of Columbia

Joseph Inslee Anderson stands as one of the most accomplished and historically significant ancestors in the Anderson line — a man whose life spanned the Revolutionary War, the birth of the United States, the founding of Tennessee, and the early years of the American government. He is not only a link in the family chain; he is a cornerstone.

Born in 1757 in White Marsh, Pennsylvania, Joseph came of age during the turbulent years leading into the American Revolution. Like thousands of young men who believed in the idea of freedom, he joined the fight for independence. His service was distinguished — he rose to the rank of **Captain in the Continental Army** and took part in some of the defining campaigns of the war.

After the Revolution, Joseph married **Patience Outlaw**, daughter of the influential Outlaw family of North Carolina and Tennessee. Through this marriage, he became connected to prominent frontier leaders and the early political shaping of the new southern territories.

☆ Builder of Tennessee

Joseph Inslee Anderson moved his family to Tennessee shortly after the war, during the early years when the region was still contested territory. His leadership and education placed him at the center of Tennessee's development. When Tennessee became a state in 1796, he was chosen to help represent it on the national stage.

★ United States Senator (1797–1815)

Joseph served an extraordinary **18 years in the United States Senate**, representing Tennessee during the presidencies of Washington, Adams, Jefferson, and Madison. His long tenure makes him one of the early pillars of Tennessee's political identity.

★ Comptroller of the U.S. Treasury

After his Senate career, Joseph was appointed **Comptroller of the Treasury**, one of the highest financial offices in the early U.S. government. He held this position from 1815 until his death in 1837, guiding the nation's financial policies during a period of rapid growth.

⭐ Legacy and Character

Joseph Inslee Anderson was known for integrity, education, and unwavering public duty. He came from a Revolutionary generation that valued honor, stability, and service. His descendants — including the Coffee County Andersons, the Oklahoma Andersons, and your own line — inherited his resilience, intelligence, and commitment to building a meaningful life.

He died in Washington City in 1837 while still serving in public office. His life forms the bedrock of your Anderson heritage: a Revolutionary soldier, a founding statesperson of Tennessee, a long-serving U.S. Senator, and a national financial leader.

⭐ Sarah Anderson

Birth: November 5, 1757, • Hopewell, Hunterdon County (now Mercer), New Jersey

Death: December 28, 1821, • Abingdon, Washington County, Virginia

Sarah Anderson was born in 1757 in the colonial community of Hopewell, New Jersey — the very same year as her brother, **Joseph Inslee Anderson**, the Revolutionary War officer and future U.S. Senator. She belonged to the generation raised on the edge of profound change: the shift from colonial dependence to the hope of American independence.

While her brothers would move into military service, law, and national politics, Sarah's life followed a quieter and more traditional path, though no less important in shaping the Anderson legacy. Like many women of her time, she became part of the westward movement that carried families from the Mid-Atlantic colonies into the developing frontier territories of Virginia, North Carolina, and eventually Tennessee.

Her death in 1821 in Abingdon, Virginia — a key early town on the Great Wagon Road and one of the gateways to the Appalachian frontier — places her directly within the migration routes used by thousands of families seeking new opportunity in the southern highlands. Many Anderson relatives traveled the same corridor on their way to what would become East Tennessee.

Though less documented in the historical record than her famous brother, Sarah Anderson's presence in the early Appalachian region confirms that the Anderson family's movement into the South was not the journey of a single line, but the combined motion of brothers, sisters, and extended kin.

Her life represents the quieter threads of the family story — the women whose strength, resilience, and day-to-day endurance created the stability upon which the more public achievements of the men often rested.

Through Sarah, the Anderson family legacy is grounded not only in public service and frontier expansion, but in the lived experiences of the early American women who helped carry the family from New Jersey into the heart of the Appalachian frontier.

☆ William Anderson

Birth: 1763 • Chester, Delaware County, Pennsylvania

Death: December 14, 1829, • Chester, Delaware County, Pennsylvania

William Anderson was born in 1763 in Chester, Pennsylvania, into the same early American world that shaped his more widely recorded siblings — including **Joseph Inslee Anderson**, the Revolutionary War officer and U.S. Senator. He belonged to the generation who grew up during the closing years of colonial life and witnessed, as young men, the upheaval of the American Revolution.

Unlike some of his brothers who would move southward into Virginia, Tennessee, and beyond, William remained rooted in Pennsylvania. Chester was one of the oldest settlements in the state, and during William's lifetime, it grew from a colonial port into a thriving early American town. His decision to remain in the region reflects the stability and deep roots that many families maintained even as others pushed westward.

Living from 1763 to 1829, William experienced the full arc of America's transformation — from the final years under British rule, through the Revolution, and into the establishment of the United States under Washington, Adams, Jefferson, and Madison. His life spanned seven decades, a time of rapid national change.

Although he did not enter political life like his brother Joseph, William represents the steadfast northern branch of the family — the part of the Anderson line that preserved its ties to Pennsylvania even as the rest of the family migrated into Tennessee, Kentucky, Missouri, and Oklahoma. His presence in the records ensures that the Anderson story is not simply one of westward movement, but one of rootedness as well.

Through William, the family maintains a firm connection to the early Mid-Atlantic settlements where the Andersons first took shape before becoming part of the American frontier story.

⭐ Margaretta Anderson

Birth: May 25, 1775, • United States

Death: October 21, 1857, • United States

Margaretta Anderson was born in 1775, in the closing years of the American colonial period. She belonged to the youngest tier of the Anderson children — the generation born as the Revolutionary War approached and the family prepared to transition into a new nation.

While her brothers' lives carried them across Pennsylvania, Tennessee, and even into government service, Margaretta's life remained undocumented, reflecting the common reality for women of her era. Yet her presence in the family structure is important. She was part of the second wave of Anderson children who bridged the old colonial world with the rising American frontier.

Her death in 1857 places her well into the 19th century, meaning she witnessed the growth of the nation through the presidencies of Washington, Jefferson, Madison, and into the expansion years that followed. Women like Margaretta often held the emotional and domestic center of early American families — raising younger siblings, maintaining household stability, and ensuring the continuity that allowed families like the Andersons to spread across the new states.

Though her personal story remains quiet in the historical record, Margaretta represents the steady, enduring strength of the Anderson family's early generations. She stands as a reminder that not all contributions were recorded in public documents — many were lived out in the daily life of family, faith, and community.

❈ Enoch Anderson Andriessen Jr.

Birth: May 4, 1698, • Long Island, Queens County, New York
Death: April 15, 1756, • Trenton, Hunterdon County, New Jersey

Enoch Anderson Andriessen Jr. represents one of the earliest roots of the Anderson family in America — a member of the Dutch American generation that helped shape early colonial life long before the Revolutionary era. Born in 1698 on Long Island, when the region still held strong Dutch and English influences, he lived in a world of early settlements, trading ports, and frontier farms.

His surname, **Andriessen**, reveals his heritage. In Dutch naming tradition, "Andriessen" means *son of Andries (Andrew)*. Over the next two generations, the family gradually shifted the name into the English form **Anderson**, reflecting their deeper integration into the growing English-speaking colonies.

By the mid-1700s, Enoch Jr. had moved into New Jersey, settling in Trenton — a developing colonial town that would later play a vital role in Revolutionary history. His arrival there helped establish the Anderson family's long presence in the Mid-Atlantic, forming the foundation upon which his sons and grandsons would build.

Enoch Jr. lived during a turbulent era marked by shifting colonial powers, conflicts on the frontier, and the first sparks of American identity. Though he died in 1756, twenty years before the Declaration of Independence, his children would carry the Anderson name directly into the Revolutionary War period and beyond.

Through him, the Anderson line transitions from its **Dutch colonial origins** into the early American world.

His descendants — including **William Anderson (1723–1778)** and **Joseph Inslee Anderson (1757–1837)** — would become soldiers, states people, pioneers, and the founders of the Tennessee branch from which Sina descends.

Enoch Anderson Andriessen Jr. stands as the bridge between two worlds:

the old Dutch settlements of early America and the rising nation that his children and grandchildren helped build.

 Mary Oakley

Birth: About 1705 • New York City, New York Colony

Death: 1767 • Trenton, Mercer County, New Jersey

Mary Oakley stands as one of the earliest maternal figures in the Anderson lineage — a woman whose life began in the bustling colonial port of New York and ended in the developing frontier communities of New Jersey. Born around 1705, during a time when New York was still marked by Dutch, English, and early American influences, she lived in one of the most important crossroads of colonial life.

Her marriage to **Enoch Anderson Andriessen Jr.** linked the Oakley family to the early Dutch American Anderson line, forming a union that would eventually lead to some of the most historically significant descendants in the lineage. Through her, the Anderson family gained deep roots in the American colonies long before the Revolution.

Mary moved with her husband into New Jersey, settling in Trenton — a community that would later gain national prominence but in her era was a developing colonial town of farms, mills, and river commerce. Her life there reflects the pattern of many early American women: steady, resilient, and essential to the growth of communities in a world shaped by both opportunity and hardship.

She raised a family whose descendants would spread across Pennsylvania, Tennessee, Virginia, and eventually the American frontier. Her son **William Anderson (1723–1778)** and grandson **Joseph Inslee Anderson (1757–1837)** would carry the family into the Revolutionary War and the founding of the United States.

Though Mary Oakley did not live to see the creation of the new nation, her life stands as a foundational chapter in the Anderson legacy.

Through her, the family's colonial, Dutch, English, and early American roots come together — forming a lineage that would one day extend to Coffee County, Oklahoma, and into the generations that follow.

❋ William Anderson

Birth: 1723 • Trenton, Hunterdon County, New Jersey
Death: 1778 • Pennsylvania

William Anderson is the earliest firmly documented patriarch of the Anderson line that leads to Tennessee. Born in 1723 in Trenton — when New Jersey was still a young colonial province — William grew up in a world shaped by frontier life, Dutch settlement, and the rising tensions that would eventually ignite the American Revolution.

He was part of the first generation to carry the family name in its fully English form, transitioning from the Dutch **Andriessen** used by his father to the American **Anderson** that would continue through all later descendants.

Like many families of the mid-1700s, William lived in the center of the colonial world of Pennsylvania and New Jersey — regions that would become crucial battlegrounds and supply centers during the Revolutionary War. He raised a large family whose lives would spread from the Mid-Atlantic into Virginia, Tennessee, and eventually across the American frontier.

William died in 1778, in the heart of the Revolutionary War. While the circumstances of his death are unknown, the year itself speaks volumes. Families across Pennsylvania faced disease, scarcity, displacement, and the hardships of war. His passing during this turbulent period reflects the cost borne by countless early American families who gave their lives, their homes, or their stability for a new nation's independence.

His legacy, however, did not end with him.

It was his children — especially **Joseph Inslee Anderson (1757–1837)** — who carried the family into public service, military distinction, and the founding of the state of Tennessee. Through William's line came soldiers, senators, pioneers, and the generations that eventually produced Sina Anderson and her descendants.

William Anderson stands as the root of the American-born Anderson family — the man whose life anchors the colonial chapter of this proud lineage.

❖ Lieutenant Colonel Richard Clough Anderson

Birth: 1725 • Anne Arundel County, Maryland
Death: January 11, 1805, • Anne Arundel County, Maryland

Lieutenant Colonel **Richard Clough Anderson** stands as one of the earliest documented military men connected to the broader Anderson heritage in colonial America. Born in 1725 in Anne Arundel County, Maryland, he belonged to the generation that witnessed the shift from frontier colonies to the beginning of American self-determination.

Richard Clough Anderson came from a region steeped in military readiness, political development, and early American leadership. Maryland in the 1700s was a place where families often balanced farming, militia duty, and public service — and Anderson clearly embodied this tradition. Rising to the rank of **Lieutenant Colonel**, he was part of the colonial militia system that protected settlements, enforced order, and prepared the colonies for the growing conflicts of the mid-18th century.

While he did not live to see the end of the Revolutionary War, his life bridged the years of rising tension that led directly to it. Men like Richard provided the military discipline, local leadership, and early patriot foundation that would shape the generation of soldiers who fought in the Revolution — including members of the Anderson family line.

He spent his life in Anne Arundel County, one of Maryland's oldest and most historically rich regions, close to the political heart of early America. His influence and military service helped shape the environment that produced future American leaders.

Though his direct connection to your Tennessee Anderson line is ancestral rather than immediate, Richard Clough Anderson represents the **military backbone** of the Anderson heritage — the tradition of service, leadership, and duty that appears repeatedly throughout the family's long history:

- in **Joseph Inslee Anderson**, the Revolutionary War captain
- in **the Tennessee settlers**, who rebuilt after the war
- and in the families who carried that strength into Oklahoma and Texas

Richard Clough Anderson's life is the foundation of that tradition — one of courage, discipline, and early American identity.

✸ Thomas Oakley Anderson

Birth: 1734 • Trenton, Mercer County, New Jersey

Death: May 29, 1805, • Newton, Sussex County, New Jersey

Thomas Oakley Anderson was born in 1734 in Trenton, New Jersey — a community that formed one of the central hubs of the early colonial world. His name clearly reflects his maternal heritage, with "Oakley" carried forward as a middle name from the Oakley line, strengthening the longstanding connection between these two early American families.

During Thomas's lifetime, New Jersey was a land of transition. Colonial farmlands and trading posts slowly transformed into communities touched by the rising spirit of independence. He lived through the French and Indian War, the birth of Revolutionary sentiment, and the emergence of the United States as a new nation. Though not recorded among the political or military men of his generation, he was part of the vital fabric of everyday colonial life — the families whose labor and perseverance laid the groundwork for the country's founding.

Thomas later settled in Newton, Sussex County, a region that formed part of New Jersey's northern frontier during the 1700s. That area, shaped by farms, mills, and early courthouse towns, played a key role in the post-Revolution expansion of the state. His move there reflects the broader migration patterns of many colonial families who sought new land and opportunity as the colonies grew.

His life spanned more than seven decades of profound change. Born under British rule and passing during the formative years of the new American republic, Thomas witnessed a world transformed. Through him, the Anderson family maintained a strong presence in New Jersey alongside the branches that migrated south toward Pennsylvania, Virginia, and eventually Tennessee.

Thomas Oakley Anderson represents the **New Jersey pillar** of the Anderson heritage — rooted in colonial life, connected through the Oakley line, and part of the early American generations that shaped the identity and endurance of the family.

✻ Joshua Anderson

Birth: October 1735, • Somerset County, New Jersey
Death: April 27, 1815, • Lower Makefield, Bucks County, Pennsylvania

Joshua Anderson was born in October 1735 in Somerset County, New Jersey — one of the oldest settled regions in the colony. He belonged to the generation of Andersons who grew up during a time of sweeping change, when small farming communities and crossroads towns were shifting into the centers of early American life.

While many branches of the Anderson family moved south into Virginia and Tennessee, Joshua represents the **Mid-Atlantic continuation** of the line — the part of the family that remained close to the New Jersey–Pennsylvania region where the Andersons first took shape in the colonies.

Lower Makefield in Bucks County, Pennsylvania, where Joshua later settled, was an important early township along the Delaware River. The area was known for its mills, river trade, and strong Quaker presence. It formed one of the main corridors for early American migration between New Jersey, Pennsylvania, and the interior frontier. Joshua's presence there reflects a life lived in the heart of the colonial and early American Northeast.

His lifespan, stretching from 1735 to 1815, carried him across the defining events of American history:

- born into British-controlled colonies
- raised during the French and Indian War
- a grown man during the Revolution
- and living into the formative decades of the new United States

Joshua Anderson's story is quieter than some of his more public relatives, but no less important. He represents the families whose daily work — farming, trade, and steady community life — supported a nation's growth. His branch helped preserve the Anderson identity in the Mid-Atlantic even as other lines pushed westward and southward into the frontier.

Through Joshua, the Anderson legacy remains deeply tied to the early American landscape of New Jersey and Pennsylvania — the colonial hearth from which so much of the family story began.

❈ Enoch Andrus Anderson

Birth: December 21, 1675, • New York City, New York Colony

Death: October 2, 1741, • Trenton, Hunterdon County, New Jersey

Enoch Andrus Anderson stands as one of the earliest known patriarchs of the American Anderson line. Born in 1675 in New

York City — when it was still transitioning from Dutch rule (New Amsterdam) into the English colony of New York — Enoch belonged to the very first generations of settlers who were shaping the identity of early America.

His original surname appears in several forms across early colonial records: **Anderson**, **Andriessen**, and **Andrus**, all rooted in the Dutch patronymic tradition meaning *"son of Andries."* These shifts in spelling reflect the blending of Dutch and English cultures in the Northeast during the late 1600s and early 1700s.

Enoch later moved to Trenton, New Jersey, a developing settlement along the Delaware River. In his era, Trenton was a growing community marked by mills, farmlands, and trade routes connecting New York, New Jersey, and Pennsylvania. His relocation there helped establish one of the earliest Anderson family roots in the Mid-Atlantic.

His life in Trenton placed the family precisely where many American families were beginning to flourish — in a region that would soon become the political and military heart of the Revolution. Although Enoch died in 1741, 35 years before the Declaration of Independence, his children and grandchildren would become part of the generation that helped shape and defend the new nation.

Through Enoch, the Anderson family becomes firmly anchored in the **earliest colonial settlements of America** — a lineage blending Dutch heritage, English influence, and the pioneering spirit that would carry the Andersons into Pennsylvania, Tennessee, Oklahoma, and into your own family line.

Enoch Andrus Anderson is the **root from which the American Anderson story truly begins**.

❈ Catherine Tryntie Opdyck

Birth: 1677 • Newtown, Queens, New York, Colonial America
Death: 1722 • Trenton, Mercer County, New Jersey, Colonial America

Catherine Tryntie Opdyck is one of the earliest matriarchs in the Anderson family line — a woman born in 1677 in Newtown, Queens, during the era when New York was still a patchwork of Dutch, English, and early American settlements.

Her heritage comes from the well-known **Opdyck (Opdycke / Updike)** family, one of the old Dutch colonial lines that helped shape the early communities of Long Island and eastern New Jersey. Families like the Opdycks were among the first to farm the land, build meeting houses, and establish the cultural foundation of what would later become New York City.

Catherine married **Enoch Andrus Anderson**, joining two strong early colonial families. Their partnership united Dutch American roots with the emerging English influence in the Northeast. Together they formed one of the earliest branches of the Anderson lineage in America.

By the early 1700s, Catherine and her husband were living in Trenton, New Jersey, a rising settlement along the Delaware River. In her era, Trenton was still a frontier town — a place of mills, ferries, and farms, situated on the main road between New York and Philadelphia. Catherine's presence there placed the Anderson family in a prime position during the decades leading up to the American Revolution.

She passed away in 1722, long before the colonies declared independence, but her children and grandchildren would carry the family into the defining events of American history. Through her, the Anderson family inherits:

- deep Dutch-colonial roots,
- early American settlement history,
- and connections to the families who helped shape the Mid-Atlantic region.

Catherine Tryntie Opdyck is the **ancestral mother** of the Anderson line in early New Jersey — a quiet but essential figure whose life began the long path that would eventually lead to Tennessee, Oklahoma, Texas, and Sina Anderson's descendants today.

✯ Enoch Anderson Andriessen Jr.

Birth: May 4, 1698, • Long Island, Queens County, New York

Death: April 15, 1756, • Trenton, Hunterdon County, New Jersey

Enoch Anderson Andriessen Jr. stands as one of the earliest firmly documented ancestors in the Anderson lineage — a bridge between the Dutch colonial world of the 1600s and the emerging English-American identity of the 1700s. Born in 1698 on Long Island, when the region was still deeply shaped by its Dutch roots, he belonged to the generation that saw New York transition from New Amsterdam into an English colony.

His surname appears in multiple early forms — **Andriessen**, **Androesen**, **Andrus**, and eventually **Anderson** — all reflecting the Dutch patronymic tradition meaning *"son of Andries."* Within two generations, this name evolved into the English spelling **Anderson**, which his children and grandchildren carried for the rest of the family's American history.

Enoch later settled in Trenton, New Jersey, a growing colonial community along the Delaware River. In the early 1700s, Trenton served as a vital link between New York and Philadelphia — a place of farms, mills, river trade, and early civic development. His move there helped establish the Anderson family's permanent presence in the Mid-Atlantic.

Enoch lived through an era marked by shifting colonial powers, frontier expansion, and rising tensions that would lay the groundwork for the American Revolution. Though he passed away in 1756 — twenty years before the Declaration of Independence — his descendants would go on to become soldiers, settlers, and political leaders in the new nation.

Through him, the Anderson line is anchored in the earliest American colonial settlements. His bloodline flows forward into:

- **William Anderson (1723–1778)**
- **Joseph Inslee Anderson (1757–1837), U.S. Senator & Revolutionary officer**

- the Tennessee Andersons,
- the Coffee County line,
- and ultimately **Sina Anderson and her descendants today**.

Enoch Anderson Andriessen Jr. is the root from which the entire American Anderson heritage grows.

❈ Joachim Von Albade Anderson (Andrieszen)

Birth: September 7, 1638, • Amsterdam, Noord-Holland, Netherlands

Death: March 11, 1674, • Elizabeth, Union County, New Jersey, Colonial America

Joachim Von Albade Anderson — also recorded as **Joachim Andrieszen** — is one of the earliest ancestors in the Anderson lineage, and the first known member of the family to immigrate to the American colonies. Born in 1638 in Amsterdam, during the height of the Dutch Golden Age, Joachim was part of a generation shaped by maritime trade, exploration, and the expanding influence of the Dutch Republic across the world.

His surname, "Andrieszen," reflects the Dutch patronymic tradition:

Andrieszen = "son of Andries (Andrew)."

Over the next two generations, this name evolved into **Anderson**, the English form that would remain with the family permanently.

Sometime before 1674, Joachim left the Netherlands and crossed the Atlantic, settling in Elizabeth, New Jersey — one of the earliest colonial towns in the region. At that time, New Jersey was contested territory, shifting between Dutch and English rule. The colony was still young, made up of scattered farms, trading posts, and Dutch and English settlers striving to establish homes in the Americas.

Joachim's arrival placed the Anderson family at the very beginning of American colonial history. Elizabeth, New Jersey, was part of the original Dutch settlements known as **New**

Netherland, and its early families became the foundation upon which later generations-built towns, counties, and eventually states.

Joachim died in 1674, just months before New Jersey became permanently English. He did not live to see the profound changes that would unfold in the next century, but his children and grandchildren became part of the American story — moving into New York, then New Jersey, and eventually into Pennsylvania and Tennessee.

Through Joachim, the Anderson line gains:

- **European origins in Amsterdam**
- **Dutch-colonial heritage in New Netherland**
- **a direct ancestral tie to the earliest settlements of the American Northeast**

His courage in crossing the ocean began the long journey that would lead — step by step — to William Anderson, to Joseph

Inslee Anderson, to the Tennessee pioneers, to Sina Anderson, and to **you**.

Joachim Von Albade Anderson is the *true Old-World root* of the Anderson Family Legacy.

❈ Emmetje "Amy" Jans Janszen

Birth: 1644 • Reusel-de Mierden, Noord-Brabant, Netherlands
Death: 1674 • Long Island, Queens County, New York, Colonial America

Emmetje "Amy" Jans Janszen is one of the earliest matriarchs of the Anderson family in America — a woman whose life began in the Dutch province of Noord-Brabant and ended in the young colonial settlements of New York. Born in 1644 in the Netherlands, Amy belonged to a generation shaped by the Dutch Golden Age, a period known for maritime exploration, thriving ports, and large numbers of families emigrating to the Americas.

Her name, **Emmetje**, is Dutch, affectionate, and feminine, while **Jans** or **Janszen** follows the Dutch patronymic pattern meaning *"daughter of Jan."* This naming tradition was common throughout the Dutch colonies and remained part of family identity until English influence gradually standardized surnames in America.

Amy married **Joachim Von Albade Anderson (Andrieszen)**, a fellow Dutch immigrant whose family name also reflected this patronymic system. Together, they became part of the early wave of Dutch settlers in New Netherland — the colonial territory that included today's New York, New Jersey, and Delaware.

While Joachim settled in Elizabeth, New Jersey, Amy's life was centered on Long Island, one of the earliest Dutch settlements. In the 1600s, Long Island was a frontier of farms, trading posts, and small Dutch communities clustered around New Amsterdam (modern New York City). It was here that their family took root in the Americas.

Amy died in 1674, the same year the Dutch permanently lost control of New Netherland to the English. Her passing marks the end of the first generation of your Anderson ancestors in America — the pioneers who crossed the Atlantic and established the family that would spread into New Jersey, Pennsylvania, Tennessee, Oklahoma, Texas, and eventually into your own modern lineage.

Through Emmetje "Amy" Jans Janszen, the Anderson Family Legacy carries:

- **Dutch colonial heritage**,
- **Old World roots from the Netherlands**,
- **a place among the first settlers of New York**,
- and the maternal foundation upon which the entire American Anderson line was built.

She stands at the beginning of the story — the mother of generations who would help shape the Americas.

✳ Enoch Andrus Anderson

Birth: December 21, 1675, • New York City, New York Colony

Death: October 2, 1741, • Trenton, Hunterdon County, New Jersey

Enoch Andrus Anderson stands as one of the earliest patriarchs of the American Anderson family — a man whose life began in the Dutch-influenced communities of New York and ended in the rising colonial settlement of Trenton, New Jersey. Born in 1675, he belonged to the generation that witnessed the transformation of New Netherland into English-controlled New York.

His surname appears in multiple forms across early records — **Andrus**, **Andriessen**, and later **Anderson** — reflecting the Dutch patronymic tradition of the time. "Andriessen" meant *"son of Andries (Andrew)."* Over the next two generations, the family adopted the English form **Anderson**, which his descendants carried into the American frontier.

At some point in his adult years, Enoch moved into New Jersey, settling in Trenton along the Delaware River. In the early 1700s, Trenton was a developing community of mills, farms, ferries, and river trade. It stood at the crossroads of the Northeast, linking New York and Philadelphia long before the Revolution. By establishing his home there, Enoch helped plant the roots of the Anderson family in one of the earliest and most historically significant colonial regions.

Enoch lived through the colonial wars, the blending of Dutch and English cultures, and the rise of the first American identity. Though he died in 1741 — decades before the Revolution — his children and grandchildren became part of the American story, spreading into Pennsylvania, Tennessee, and beyond.

Through him, the Anderson family enters the documented history of early America.

His life provides the bridge between the Old World Dutch roots and the American identity that his descendants, including **William Anderson (1723–1778)** and **Joseph Inslee Anderson (1757–1837)**, would carry into the founding of the new nation.

Enoch Andrus Anderson is the **true early-colonial root** of your Anderson line.

Note on the Anderson Children of These Generation

The historical records for this early branch of the Anderson family contain several names that appear multiple times, are inconsistent across sources, or lack clear documentation. To maintain accuracy and avoid confusion, only the children with reliable, well-supported records have been included in this book.

Additional names appear in some genealogical lists, but due to uncertainties in spelling, dates, and family placement, they have been respectfully omitted until further evidence can confirm their place in the lineage.

✹ Closing Note – The Old-World Ends, The New World Begins

With **Enoch Andrus Anderson (1675–1741)** and **Emmetje "Amy" Jans Janszen (1644–1674)**, this line of the Anderson family reaches its final recorded generation before their arrival in America. These ancestors were born in the Netherlands and the Dutch colonial settlements of New York, living during a time when surnames were still shifting, records were sparse, and families crossed an ocean in search of a new beginning.

Before this point, documentation becomes limited, fragmented, and uncertain.

For that reason, this book respectfully ends the line **with the first generation who lived and died on American soil.**

Their courage, migration, and resilience form the foundation of everything that followed —

from the early days of New Jersey and Pennsylvania,

to the Tennessee settlers,

to Sina Anderson,

and to the generations alive today.

What lies before them belongs to the Old World;

what comes after them belongs to the American story of the Anderson family.

Good Family Line

John Edward Good, Sr.

Born: *1810 — Sauratown, Stokes County, North Carolina, USA*

Died: *1880 — Roff Town, Pontotoc County, Oklahoma*

Profile:

John Edward Good, Sr. was born in the rolling hills of Stokes County, North Carolina, during the early Federal period. Like many families of that era, the Goods traveled west across the American frontier, following the openings through Tennessee, Arkansas, and into Indian Territory. By the late 1800s, John Edward had settled at Roff Town in what is now Pontotoc County, Oklahoma.

He lived through enormous shifts in American history — from the post-Revolution era through Removal, the Civil War, and the settlement of early Oklahoma Territory. His descendants became woven into the Anderson, Good, and Roberts family lines.

Sina's second Husband:

John Edward Good Sr.

Born: 1810 – North Carolina, USA

Died: 1880 – Roff Town, Pontotoc County, Oklahoma, USA

Relation: Father of Edward Good (the second husband of Sina Anderson [Anderson Good])

John Edward Good Sr. was a pioneer of quiet dignity and enduring faith. Born in the early years of the nineteenth century, his life bridged the rugged lands of North Carolina and the open territories of Oklahoma. He guided his family through seasons of change with patience, integrity, and an unwavering belief in hard work and devotion to home. Through his son

Edward Good's marriage to Sina Anderson, the Good family became woven into the Anderson heritage — a union that joined two lines of strength, service, and Light across generations.

Delila A. Ellison Good

Born: 1823 – Tennessee, USA

Died: 1880 – Hillsboro, Coffee County, Tennessee, USA

Relation: First wife of John Edward Good Sr.; Mother of Edward Good (the second husband of Sina Anderson [Anderson Good])

Delila A. Ellison Good was a woman of faith and endurance, whose quiet devotion shaped the early Good family line. Born in the hills of Tennessee, she lived a life rooted in family and guided by steadfast belief. Her marriage to John Edward Good Sr. brought forth a lineage of integrity and perseverance that would later join with the Andersons through her son Edward Good. Though her years ended in Hillsboro, the strength of her spirit continued westward through her children, uniting two families in purpose and Light.

Children: 1st married:

Griffin M. Good

Born: 1844 – Tennessee, USA

Died: November 10, 1863 – Chicago, Cook County, Illinois, USA

Relation: Son of John Edward Good Sr. and Delila A. Ellison Good; Brother of Edward Good

Griffin M. Good lived during one of the most turbulent chapters in American history. Born in Tennessee, he came of age as the nation divided, and his path led him far from home into the trials of the Civil War. Passing away in 1863 in Chicago, his life was brief yet marked by courage and duty. Through his sacrifice, the Good family's legacy of service was forever written into the story of the Anderson–Good line. Though his years were few, his name stands among those who gave their lives in the hope of peace and unity for generations to come.

Sarah Jane Good

Born: February 27, 1848 – Wilson County, Tennessee, USA

Died: May 20, 1903 – Marshall County, Oklahoma, USA

Relation: Daughter of John Edward Good Sr. and Delila A. Ellison Good; Stepdaughter of Sina Anderson (Anderson Good)

Sarah Jane Good grew up amid the hills of Tennessee and journeyed west as the frontier opened. Through faith and perseverance, she carried forward the Good family's quiet strength into the lands that would become Oklahoma. Her life bridged two families and two eras — the Tennessee homeland of her birth and the new frontier of her later years. As the stepdaughter of Sina Anderson (Anderson Good), she became part of the enduring union between the Good and Anderson lines, her story joining the broader heritage of courage, endurance, and Light that defines their shared legacy.

Thomas Bailey Good

Born: February 1850 – Wilson County, Tennessee, USA

Died: Before 1930 – Coffee County, Tennessee, USA

Relation: Son of John Edward Good Sr. and Delila A. Ellison Good; Stepson of Sina Anderson (Anderson Good)

Thomas Bailey Good was born amid the farmlands of Wilson County, Tennessee, and spent much of his life near the family's ancestral roots in Coffee County. A man of quiet diligence, he carried forward the work and values instilled by his parents, John Edward Good Sr., and Delila Ellison Good. Through his stepmother, Sina Anderson (Anderson Good), his life became interwoven with the Anderson line, joining two families whose histories shaped the heart of early Tennessee. His story stands as a reminder of steadfast faith, humble labor, and the enduring ties of family that stretch across generations.

John Edward Good Jr.

Born: March 21, 1852 – Franklin County, Tennessee, USA

Died: March 5, 1931 – Roff, Pontotoc County, Oklahoma, USA

Relation: Son of John Edward Good Sr. and Delila A. Ellison Good; Stepson of Sina Anderson (Anderson Good)

John Edward Good Jr. was part of the generation that carried the Good family westward from the hills of Tennessee into the open plains of Oklahoma. Born in Franklin County, he grew up with the strong values of faith and perseverance that marked the Good name. His later years in Roff, Pontotoc County — the same community where Sina Anderson (Anderson Good) would one day rest — reflected the quiet continuation of family bonds through time and distance. Through his life, the Good legacy remained rooted in service, faith, and devotion, joining harmoniously with the Anderson line to form one enduring heritage of Light and remembrance.

Martha Louisa "Mattie" Good

Born: February 15, 1854 – Franklin County, Tennessee, USA

Died: June 16, 1897 – Coffee County, Tennessee, USA

Relation: Daughter of John Edward Good Sr. and Delila A. Ellison Good; Stepson of Sina Anderson (Anderson Good)

Martha Louisa "Mattie" Good was born in the heart of Tennessee, where the Good and Anderson families' stories intertwined. Known for her warmth and gentle spirit, she embodied the quiet strength of her lineage. Though her life was brief, her years were filled with faith, family, and devotion to the land she called home. Her passing in Coffee County closed a chapter of the early Good family's Tennessee years — a chapter remembered through love, legacy, and the unbroken bond between two families joined by Light.

Nancy Good

Born: About 1856 – Franklin County, Tennessee, USA

Died: Before 1870

Relation: Daughter of John Edward Good Sr. and Delila A. Ellison Good; Stepson of Sina Anderson (Anderson Good)

Nancy Good lived only a brief time, but her name remains a gentle part of the Good family story. Born during the family's years in Franklin County, Tennessee, she was one of the youngest children of John Edward and Delila Ellison Good. Though her life ended before the family's later move west, her memory lives through her siblings who carried the Good legacy into Oklahoma and beyond. In remembrance, she stands as one of the many early lights in a lineage built upon love, faith, and the eternal bond of family.

Robert Edward Good

Born: May 1859 – Elk River, Franklin County, Tennessee, USA

Died: 1954 – Hobart, Kiowa County, Oklahoma, USA

Relation: Son of John Edward Good Sr. and Delila A. Ellison Good; Brother of Edward Good (the second husband of Sina Anderson [Anderson Good])

Robert Edward Good was born along the Elk River in Franklin County, Tennessee, during the final years of his family's life in the South. A man of quiet faith and resolve, he journeyed west as part of the generation that helped settle the Oklahoma

territories. Through his life's work and steady character, he carried forward the spirit of his parents, John Edward, and Delila Good. His long life spanned a century of change, and through it all he upheld the family's devotion to honesty, service, and kinship. His presence in Oklahoma linked the past and future of the Good lineage, ensuring that the Light of his family's name endured across time and place.

Edwards Father:

Henry Goode

Born: *1784 — Stokes County, North Carolina, USA*

Died: *About 1840 — Montgomery County, Tennessee*

Father of: *John Edward Good, Sr. (1810–1880)*

Profile:

Henry Goode was born in 1784 in Stokes County, North Carolina, during the young years of the new United States. He came of age in the early frontier period when families were moving westward seeking land, opportunity, and stability after the Revolution.

Like many early North Carolina families, the Goode line followed the migration routes into Tennessee. By the 1830s, Henry had settled in Montgomery County, Tennessee, one of the developing regions along the Cumberland settlements. His life reflects the early pioneer movement — from the foothills of North Carolina into the growing communities of Middle Tennessee.

Henry's legacy continued through his son, **John Edward Good, Sr.**, who later carried the family farther west into Arkansas and Indian Territory. This makes Henry one of the key ancestral roots of the Good–Anderson line.

Phoebe Blackburn Goode

Born: *30 April 1790 — Stokes County, North Carolina, USA*
Died: *15 April 1851 — Stokes County, North Carolina, USA*

Wife of: *Henry Goode (1784–ca.1840)*

Grandmother of: *John Edward Good, Sr.*

Great-Grandmother of: *Robert Edward Good*

Profile:

Phoebe Blackburn was born in 1790 in Stokes County, North Carolina, into one of the early families of the region. She lived her entire life in Stokes County, remaining close to the roots of the Blackburn and Goode families even as many relatives began moving westward into Tennessee and beyond.

She married **Henry Goode**, and together they raised their family in the foothills of North Carolina during a time of dramatic change — from the post-Revolution years through the opening of western lands. While Henry later appears in Tennessee, Phoebe remained in North Carolina, close to her kin and the early settlements that shaped the family's identity.

Her steady presence and long life created a sturdy foundation for the generations that followed. Through her son, **John Edward Good, Sr.**, and her descendants in Tennessee,

Arkansas, and Indian Territory, Phoebe stands as a central matriarch in the Good family line.

William Goode

Born: *1809 — Stokes County, North Carolina, USA*

Died: *Before 1838 — Stokes County, North Carolina*

Son of: *Henry Goode (1784–ca.1840) and Phoebe Blackburn Goode (1790–1851)*

Brother of: *John Edward Good, Sr. (1810–1880)*

Profile:

William Goode was born in 1809 in Stokes County, North Carolina, into the early Goode–Blackburn pioneer families of the region. He was one of the older sons of **Henry Goode** and **Phoebe Blackburn**, raised in the rolling farmland between the Dan and Yadkin Rivers.

William's life was short — records show he died before 1838. His early passing came during a time when illness, accidents, and the hardships of frontier life claimed many young men. Though his life did not extend into the later family migrations, William remains an important part of the Good lineage. His siblings carried the line forward into Tennessee, Arkansas, and eventually Indian Territory.

His younger brother, **John Edward Good, Sr.**, continued the family's westward movement, becoming the ancestor of the Oklahoma Good line connected to Sina Anderson's descendants.

Thomas Goode

Born: *1810 — Stokes County, North Carolina, USA*

Died: *1897 — Belews Creek, Forsyth County, North Carolina, USA*

Son of: *Henry Goode (1784–ca.1840) and Phoebe Blackburn Goode (1790–1851)*

Brother of: *John Edward Good, Sr. (1810–1880)*

Uncle of: *Robert Edward Good*

Profile:

Thomas Goode was born in 1810 in Stokes County, North Carolina, into the pioneer Goode–Blackburn family line. Unlike several of his brothers who traveled west into Tennessee and Indian Territory, Thomas remained in North Carolina, carrying on the family name in their home region.

He lived most of his life in the Belews Creek area, now part of Forsyth County, a community formed from early Stokes and Surry County settlements. Thomas lived a long life — reaching 87 years — and witnessed the transformation of North Carolina from early frontier settlements into established towns and counties. His presence kept a strong branch of the Goode family rooted in the original homeland even as other branches moved westward.

Through his siblings, including **John Edward Good, Sr.**, Thomas stands as part of the ancestral foundation of the Good line connected to the Anderson and Sina families.

John Edward Good, Sr.

Born: *1810 — Sauratown, Stokes County, North Carolina, USA*

Died: *1880 — Roff Town, Pontotoc County, Oklahoma*

Son of: *Henry Goode (1784–ca.1840) and Phoebe Blackburn Goode (1790–1851)*

Father of: *Robert Edward Good*

*Grandfather of the Oklahoma Good line

Profile:

John Edward Good, Sr. was born in 1810 in Sauratown, Stokes County, North Carolina — one of the earliest centers of Goode and Blackburn family settlement. He grew up among the foothills and farming communities of Stokes County before joining the westward movement that defined so many early American families.

John's life carried the Goode line out of North Carolina and into the expanding frontier. By the mid-1800s, he moved through Tennessee and Arkansas, eventually settling in Indian Territory.

His final home was **Roff Town in Pontotoc County, Oklahoma**, where he became one of the early settlers of the region.

He lived through some of America's greatest periods of change — frontier expansion, the formation of new states, and the early generations of Oklahoma Territory. Through his son, **Robert Edward Good**, John became the founding ancestor of the Good family branch that later intertwined with the Anderson and Sina line.

John Edward Good, Sr.'s life marks the beginning of the Oklahoma Good legacy — a line defined by resilience, migration, and strong family ties that carried forward for generations.

Solomon Good

Born: *1815 — Stokes County, North Carolina, USA*
Died: *Unknown*

Son of: *Henry Goode (1784–ca.1840) and Phoebe Blackburn Goode (1790–1851)*

Brother of: *John Edward Good, Sr. (1810–1880)*

Profile:

Solomon Good was born in 1815 in Stokes County, North Carolina, one of the younger sons of **Henry Goode** and **Phoebe Blackburn Goode**. Like his brothers, he was raised in the foothills of northern North Carolina, where the Goode and Blackburn families had deep early roots.

While several of his siblings moved west into Tennessee, Arkansas, and Indian Territory, the historical record for Solomon is limited. His later life, movements, and place of death remain unknown, which was common for early 1800s families whose records were lost to time, courthouse fires, or migration beyond established settlements.

Even with the limited documentation, Solomon remains an important part of the Goode family foundation — one of the branches that grew from Henry and Phoebe, forming the ancestral roots of the Good line that would eventually connect with the Anderson and Sina family paths.

1. Thomas Goode Jr. (1750–1834)

Born: 1750 • Essex County, Virginia

Died: 1834 • Surry County, North Carolina

Relationship: *Paternal grandfather of the husband of your 2nd great-grandaunt.*

But for our book's structure, he is also the **patriarchal root** of the Good line that eventually merges into the Anderson family through Sina's descendants.

Known Facts:

- Born in colonial Virginia, in the region where many Goode families were established by the mid-1700s.
- Migrated southward into **Surry County, North Carolina**, part of the early movement of Virginia frontier families.

- His lifespan covers the entire Revolutionary era and the early nationhood period.
- By his death in 1834, multiple branches of the Goode family had moved further west into **Stokes County**, then ultimately on into **Pontotoc County and Indian Territory**, where your direct Good ancestors appear.

Children (relevant to your line):

- **Henry Goode (1784–abt.1840)** — the direct ancestor your line follows
  - Married **Phoebe Blackburn (1790–1851)**
  - Their children include:
    - **John Edward Good Sr.** (1810–1880) → your connecting line
    - **William Goode (1809–bef.1838)**
    - **Thomas Goode (1810–1897)**
    - **Solomon Good (1815–??)**

Wife:

1. Nancy Elizabeth Beasley (1756–1795)

Born: 1756 • Caroline County, Virginia

Died: 1795 • Stokes County, North Carolina

Spouse: Thomas Goode Jr. (1750–1834)

Relationship: *Matriarchal ancestor in the early Good–Beasley union that leads into the Good line connected with Sina Anderson's extended family.*

About Nancy Elizabeth Beasley

Nancy was born in **Caroline County, Virginia**, a region known in the mid-1700s for established colonial families, tobacco farms, and early migration routes leading south. Her marriage to **Thomas Goode Jr.** linked two long-standing Virginia lineages and became the root of the Good family's later westward movement.

During her lifetime, Nancy relocated with Thomas into what would become **Stokes County, North Carolina**, part of the waves of Virginia families seeking new farmland after the

Revolution. She passed away in 1795, several years before large segments of the family began migrating toward Surry and then into the growing frontier regions of what would later become **Oklahoma**.

Children (Relevant to Your Line):

Nancy and Thomas's known children include:

- **Henry Goode**

    Born: 1784 • Stokes County, North Carolina

    Died: abt. 1840 • Montgomery County, Tennessee

    Married: **Phoebe Blackburn (1790–1851)**

    Line continues through:

    - **John Edward Good Sr. (1810–1880)** → Your connecting Good/Anderson branch

Nancy's early passing meant she did not witness the later migration of her children and grandchildren into Tennessee, then Indian Territory — but she is the **matriarchal root** of the branch that eventually becomes part of Sina Anderson's ancestral story.

Children:

Mary "Polly" Goode (1776–1855)

Born: 22 August 1776 • Stokes County, North Carolina

Died: 21 August 1855 • Campbellsburg, Washington County, Indiana

Relationship: *Aunt of the husband of your 2nd great-grandaunt.*

In the broader family history, Mary represents an **older branch of the same Goode line** that produced Henry Goode (1784) and eventually the Good ancestors who merge with the Anderson family.

About Mary "Polly" Goode

Mary Polly Goode was born the same year the United States declared independence — **1776** — in Stokes County, North

Carolina. She was part of the early Goode families who settled the region while it was still rugged by frontier land.

Her life reflects a classic Appalachian migration pattern:

1. **Virginia → North Carolina** with her parents (Thomas Goode Sr. or Jr. lineage)
2. Then **North Carolina → Indiana** in her later years — a common route families took as new territories opened.

By the mid-1800s, she was living in **Campbellsburg, Washington County, Indiana**, where she died one day before her 79th birthday.

Family Context

Mary Polly was:

- A **sibling in the generation before Henry Goode (1784)**
- Part of the larger Good/Goode family network spreading from colonial Virginia into the Carolinas

- A representative of the **Indiana branch**, which is separate from but related to the Tennessee/Oklahoma branch your direct ancestors belong to

Although Mary Polly herself is not a direct ancestor, her help shows:

- **How wide the Good family spread**
- How interconnected the lineages were
- How both the Indiana and Tennessee/Oklahoma branches share the same roots

Why She Matters in Your Book

Even though your line descends through **Henry Goode (1784)**, the siblings, and cousins — like Polly — show how the Good family expanded and shaped settlement patterns across early America.

She adds **depth**, **movement**, and **historical context** to the Good section of the *Sina Anderson* book.

Joseph Goode (1778–Unknown)

Born: 1778 • Surry County, North Carolina

Died: Unknown

Relationship: Member of the older Goode generation; sibling/kin to the line that leads directly into Henry Goode (1784) and the Good ancestors tied to Sina Anderson's extended family.

About Joseph Goode

Joseph was born in **Surry County, North Carolina**, during the period when the Goode family was firmly established across the border regions of Surry and Stokes counties. This was a transitional time in early American history — just before the Revolutionary War — when many Virginia families, including the Goodes, were migrating south to find new land.

While little is recorded about Joseph's later life, his presence in this generation helps map out the **broader sibling network** that formed the early Goode branches. Families in this region often stayed close together, working land, forming early communities, and later pushing westward into Tennessee, Indiana, Kentucky, and eventually Indian Territory.

Joseph represents the **unrecorded but essential backbone** of large frontier families:

- His exact death date is unknown
- No formal burial record has been located
- But census, land, and community patterns show he was part of the same cluster of siblings that included:
    - **Mary "Polly" Goode (1776–1855)**
    - **Henry Goode (1784–abt.1840)** → your direct line
    - And several other children of **Thomas Goode Jr. and Nancy Beasley**

Why He Matters in the Book

Even when details are missing, ancestors like Joseph help show:

- The size of frontier families

- The network of kin that shaped moves from Virginia to North Carolina
- The shared roots of multiple Good branches — one that moved toward Indiana, one toward Tennessee and Oklahoma

Including Joseph makes the Good Line more complete and historically grounded.

George Goode (1780–Unknown)

Born: 1780 • Surry County, North Carolina

Died: Unknown

Relationship: Member of the same Goode sibling generation as Joseph, Mary Polly, and Henry Goode. He is part of the extended family branch that forms the foundation of the Good line eventually connected with Sina Anderson's descendants.

About George Goode

George Goode was born in **1780** in Surry County, North Carolina — during the early settlement years when the Goode family was expanding from Virginia into the Carolina frontier. His life began at a time when the region was just becoming organized, with new farms being carved from wilderness and families establishing long-lasting roots.

Little is documented about George's adult life, but this was common for rural men of the late 1700s–early 1800s who:

- Worked family land
- Appeared only sporadically in tax rolls or early censuses
- Traveled or relocated without leaving clear paper trails
- Built the community foundations later generations grew from

His presence in this generation helps reconstruct the **full family unit** of Thomas Goode Jr. and Nancy Beasley's children.

Likely Siblings (Based on age & locality):

George is part of the same sibling group that includes:

- **Mary "Polly" Goode (1776–1855)**
- **Joseph Goode (1778–Unknown)**
- **Henry Goode (1784–abt.1840)** → your direct ancestral line
- Other siblings not yet fully documented, but associated by census and location

Why George Belongs in the Book

Even when details are sparse, George's inclusion strengthens the narrative by:

- Showing the **size and stability** of the early Goode family
- Demonstrating how many branches rose from the same North Carolina roots
- Providing context for how the Good line eventually split into:
    - The **Indiana branch**
    - The **Tennessee → Oklahoma branch** (your line)

Each sibling helps tell the full story of how the Good family grew, divided, and spread across early America.

Henry Goode (1784 – abt. 1840)

Born: 1784 • Stokes County, North Carolina

Died: About 1840 • Montgomery County, Tennessee

Relationship: *Father-in-law of your 2nd great grandaunt; direct ancestor within the Good line that joins the Anderson family network.*

About Henry Goode

Henry Goode represents one of the **most important transitional figures** in your Good lineage. Born in **Stokes County, North Carolina**, he was part of the larger Goode family descending from Thomas Goode Jr. and Nancy Beasley — the early Virginia-to-Carolina settlers.

Where earlier Goode generations remained in the Surry/Stokes region, Henry was part of the **westward migration** into:

- **Tennessee**, then
- Into regions that would become **Oklahoma Territory** through his children and grandchildren.

Henry's move to **Montgomery County; Tennessee** marks the beginning of a new chapter for the Good family: the bridge between their colonial Virginia roots and their later frontier life.

Marriage

Henry married:

Phoebe Blackburn (1790–1851)

Born in Stokes County, NC, Phoebe was part of another long-established Carolina family. Their marriage united two frontier lines and produced children who would later become central to both Tennessee and Oklahoma settlements.

Children (relevant to your line):

Henry and Phoebe's known children include:

- **John Edward Good Sr. (1810–1880)**

  Born: Sauratown, Stokes County, NC

  Died: Roff Town, Pontotoc County, Oklahoma

  → **Your direct Good ancestor who ties into the extended Anderson lineage**

- **William Goode (1809–bef.1838)**

- **Thomas Goode (1810–1897)** — same birth year as John

  Edward, twins or close in age

- **Solomon Good (1815–??)**

- Other children not fully documented but present in early census clusters

Historical Context

Henry lived during a major movement of families from the North Carolina foothills into:

- **Middle Tennessee** (1800–1830)
- **Indian Territory/Oklahoma** (1830s–1850s through his children)

His death around **1840** places him in the era just before many Good descendants began moving into what would later become **Pontotoc County, Oklahoma** — the heart of your family's later generations.

Why Henry Is Central to the Book

Henry is the **turning point**:

- The generation that leaves the Carolinas
- The generation that begins the Tennessee chapter
- The ancestor whose children eventually become early settlers in **Oklahoma Territory**, where the Good and Anderson families later connect

In the story of Sina Anderson, Henry's life marks the **geographical and generational crossroads** that leads directly to the families whose lines converge in your heritage.

Thomas Goode Sr. (1716–1789)

Born: 1716 • Essex County, Virginia

Died: 9 March 1789 • Stokes/Surry County, North Carolina

Relationship: Foundational patriarch of the Goode line. Ancestor of Thomas Goode Jr. and the entire Carolina branch that eventually connects into the Good–Anderson heritage.

About Thomas Goode Sr.

Thomas Goode Sr. stands at the **beginning of the documented Goode line** that later appears in Stokes and Surry Counties, North Carolina. Born in **1716 in Essex County, Virginia**, he was part of the early colonial Goode families that had settled in the Tidewater and Piedmont regions.

During the mid-1700s, as land in eastern Virginia became increasingly divided, many families pushed south and west in search of new farmland. Thomas Sr. was among these early movers, establishing himself and his family in:

- **Surry County**,

- Later divided into **Stokes County**, North Carolina.

This relocation placed the Goode family along the frontier line of the growing colonies — a place where farms were carved from hardwood forests and new communities formed through hard labor and close family bonds.

Family & Legacy

Thomas Sr. is believed to be the father of:

- **Thomas Goode Jr. (1750–1834)** → the ancestor who continues your Good line
- Other early children who helped establish the family in Stokes/Surry County

His descendants became:

- Pioneers in North Carolina (Stokes, Surry)
- Migrants into Tennessee (Montgomery County)
- Early settlers in Oklahoma Territory (Pontotoc County)

Thomas Sr.'s move from Virginia into North Carolina is the **first major migration** for your Good ancestors — the beginning of the journey that eventually entwines with the Anderson family line.

Historical Context

By the time of his death in **1789**:

- America had just won independence
- North Carolina had recently become a state (1789)
- The Goode family was firmly rooted in the Stokes/Surry region
- His children and grandchildren were already spreading through the foothills and beginning the next migration westward

Thomas Sr. lived through:

- Colonial settlement

- The French & Indian War
- The American Revolution
- And the founding years of the United States

His life bookends a time of enormous transformation — and through his descendants, that transformation continues all the way into your Oklahoma branches.

Wife:

Mary Reynolds (1728–1819)

Born: August 1728 • Essex County, Virginia

Died: September 1819 • Stokes County, North Carolina

Spouse: Thomas Goode Sr. (1716–1789)

Relationship: Foundational matriarch of the Goode line; mother of Thomas Goode Jr. and ancestor of the entire Carolina-to-Tennessee Good lineage that ultimately connects with the Anderson family.

About Mary Reynolds

Mary Reynolds was born in **1728 in Essex County, Virginia**, a region filled with some of the oldest colonial families in America. Raised during the era of large plantations, tobacco culture, and early settlement expansion, Mary represented the strong, stable Virginia roots that would anchor the Goode family for generations.

In the mid-1700s, she married **Thomas Goode Sr.**, and together they joined the migration trend that carried many Virginia families southward into the frontier edges of **North Carolina**.

Migration & Family Establishment

By the 1760s–1770s, Mary and Thomas were among the early families settling the region that would later be divided into **Surry** and **Stokes** Counties. They were part of the first wave of settlers carving homesteads from forestland, forming the earliest communities, and establishing family networks that would dominate the area for decades.

Mary lived a remarkably long life for her time — **91 years**, spanning from the early colonial era to the post-Revolutionary frontier world. She lived:

- Before the French & Indian War
- Through the entire American Revolution
- Into the early United States
- Watching her children, grandchildren, and great-grandchildren spread across the Carolinas and into Tennessee

Her life is one of the longest of any early Good ancestors you

Capt. Richard Goode (1749–1801)

Born: 1749 • Rappahannock River Region, Virginia

Died: 20 April 1801 • Abingdon, Wythe County, Virginia

Also Known As: *"Captain Richard Goode"*

Relationship: A cousin/parallel branch of the Carolina Goode family; not in the direct line, but part of the **larger Goode network** that originated in colonial Virginia.

About Capt. Richard Goode

Capt. Richard Goode was born along the **Rappahannock River**, one of the earliest and most heavily settled colonial regions in Virginia. Many Goode families in the mid-1700s lived, worked, and intermarried along this river basin, forming the broad ancestral network from which your Carolina Goode line also descends.

Richard earned the title **"Captain,"** which reflects either:

- A commission in the **Virginia Militia**, or
- Service during the **Revolutionary War** era

  (many men of his age were involved in local militia companies)

He represents the **Virginia-stay branch** of the Goode family, those who remained in the eastern part of the state while other branches (like yours) migrated into **North Carolina, Tennessee, Indiana, and eventually Oklahoma.**

Migration & Life

By the late 1700s, Richard had moved southwest into the Appalachian region, settling in:

- **Abingdon,**
- **Wythe County**, Virginia—

  an important frontier town on the early Wilderness Road.

This area was a major crossroads for settlers heading into Kentucky, Tennessee, and Ohio Valley. Richard lived at the center of this movement, and his presence shows how widely the Goode families spread across the early American frontier.

Family Context

Capt. Richard is part of the **extended Goode kin network**, which includes:

- The **Essex/Rappahannock County roots** (directly tied to your Thomas Goode Sr. and Mary Reynolds)
- The **Carolina migration lines** (your direct ancestors)
- The **Appalachian Virginia lines**, where Richard settled

While Richard is not in your direct line, including him in the Good section adds depth, showing:

- The military service tradition in the family
- The wide geographic spread of Goode descendants

- The shared Virginia origins of

-

- ## Thomas Goode Jr. (1750–1834)

Born: 1750 • Essex County, Virginia

Died: 1834 • Surry County, North Carolina

Parents: Thomas Goode Sr. (1716–1789) & Mary Reynolds (1728–1819)

Spouse: Nancy Elizabeth Beasley (1756–1795)

Relationship: Direct ancestor and father of **Henry Goode (1784)** — the central connecting line leading to the Good-Anderson heritage.

About Thomas Goode Jr.

Thomas Goode Jr. was born in **Essex County, Virginia**, into a well-established colonial family with deep ties to the early Tidewater region. Like many families of his generation, he moved southward with his parents during the mid-1700s, settling in the foothill lands of **Surry County, North Carolina**, which later became part of **Stokes County**.

Thomas Jr. became the foundational figure for the **North Carolina branch** of the Goode family. Through him, the line transitions from Virginia plantation life into the rugged, self-sufficient frontier settlements of the Carolina backcountry.

He lived to the remarkable age of **84**, witnessing:

- The French & Indian War
- The American Revolution
- The founding of the United States
- The settlement and gradual expansion of the frontier

His long life allowed him to watch his children and grandchildren anchor the Goode family firmly in North Carolina before later generations pushed onward into Tennessee and Indian Territory.

Marriage & Family

Thomas Jr. married:

Nancy Elizabeth Beasley (1756–1795)

Their union produced multiple children who formed the core of the early Surry/Stokes Goode family.

Children (relevant to your line):

- **Henry Goode (1784–abt.1840)** → your direct ancestor
- Mary "Polly" Goode (1776–1855)
- Joseph Goode (1778–unknown)
- George Goode (1780–unknown)
- Other children suggested by census clusters

Henry's move into Tennessee, and his son's move into Oklahoma Territory, trace directly back through Thomas Jr.'s Carolina homestead.

Thomas Jr.'s Legacy

Thomas Jr. stands as the **patriarch** of the Carolina-to-Tennessee branch of the Goode family. His descendants would:

- Populate **Stokes & Surry Counties** for decades
- Move into **Montgomery County, Tennessee**
- Push further west into **Pontotoc County, Oklahoma Territory**
- Eventually merge into the extended **Anderson family line**

His life marks the transition from colonial Virginia roots to the frontier Carolina settlements that shaped the Good family's future path.

George Goode (1751 – after 1810)

Born: 1751 • St. Anne's Parish, Essex County, Virginia

Died: After 1810 • Surry/Stokes County, North Carolina

Relationship: A member of the older Goode generation who migrated from Virginia into the North Carolina frontier. A brother or close cousin of **Thomas Goode Jr. (1750–1834)**. Part of the extended ancestral circle surrounding the direct Good line.

About George Goode

George Goode was born in **St. Anne's Parish**, one of the oldest settled areas of Essex County, Virginia. This parish was a crucial point for early plantation families, including the Goodes, who had been living in the region since the late 1600s.

Like many of his kin, George joined the southward migration into the foothills of **North Carolina**, following the same route and settling in the same region as the direct ancestors of Good line.

By the early 1800s, he was living in:

- **Surry County**

- Later part of **Stokes County**

where numerous Goode households appear together in census clusters, land grants, and tax lists. Such clustering strongly suggests family groups migrating and settling together.

Historical Presence

George is documented as still living **after 1810**, placing him:

- In the post-Revolution years
- During the early organization of Stokes County
- In the same community as Thomas Jr., Henry, and the next generation of Goodes

His life spans the same major historical periods as the rest of the family — the Revolutionary War, the founding of the new nation, and the westward migration era.

- He establishes that the family was not a single isolated line, but part of a broad and interconnected Virginia-Carolina migration

Eleanor "Nelly" Goode (1753–1840)

Born: 1753 • St. Anne's Parish, Essex County, Virginia

Died: December 1840 • Stokes County, North Carolina

Relationship: Member of the same Virginia-born sibling generation as **Thomas Goode Jr. (1750)** and **George Goode (1751)**. Part of the extended Goode family whose move from Virginia to North Carolina shaped the environment of your direct ancestors.

About Eleanor "Nelly" Goode

Eleanor—often called "Nelly"—was born in **St. Anne's Parish**, the same Virginia parish that produced several generations of Goode family members. This parish was a hub of early Virginia settlement, and many Goode children born there in the mid-1700s later migrated south toward North Carolina.

Nelly represents the **women's side** of that migration—those who helped anchor the family through marriage alliances, household leadership, and community building.

Like her brothers and cousins, she joined the large Goode movement into:

- **Surry County, North Carolina**,
- And remained there after it subdivided into **Stokes County**.

She spent the rest of her long life in the Carolina foothills, passing away in **December 1840** at approximately **87 years old**.

Historical Context

Nelly's lifespan is extraordinary for her era. She lived through:

- Colonial Virginia
- The French & Indian War
- The American Revolution
- The birth of the United States
- The era of frontier expansion into Tennessee and Kentucky
- The early formation of Stokes County (1789)
- The beginning of the migration into what would become Oklahoma Territory (her nephews and their descendants later made this move)

Her life is a living bridge from **early colonial society** to the dawn of the American frontier world.

Family Connections

Eleanor "Nelly" Goode is part of the same sibling cluster as:

- **Thomas Goode Jr. (1750–1834)** → Your direct ancestor

- **George Goode (1751–aft.1810)**
- Other siblings born in Essex County who migrated together

Her presence confirms the **tight network** of Goode families who moved as large kin groups from Virginia into the North Carolina foothills. These networks are what allowed your direct ancestors—Thomas Jr., then Henry, then John Edward Good—to thrive and grow.

- Nelly is demonstrating that the family migration was not only fathers and sons—it was entire households, including daughters, sisters, and extended kin
- Strengthening the understanding of how wide the Good family presence was in early Stokes County

Capt. William Goode (1755 – after 1840)

Born: 1755 • St. Anne's Parish, Essex County, Virginia

Died: After 1840 • Stokes County, North Carolina

Also Known As: *"Captain William Goode"*

Relationship: Member of the same Virginia-born sibling generation as **Thomas Goode Jr. (1750)**, **George Goode (1751)**, and **Eleanor "Nelly" Goode (1753)**. Part of the extended Goode kin group who migrated from Virginia into the Carolina frontier.

About Capt. William Goode

William Goode was born in **St. Anne's Parish**, Essex County—one of the oldest and most stable colonial regions in Virginia. Like his siblings, he grew up during a time of profound political and social change, witnessing the early stirrings of what would eventually become the American Revolution.

William earned the title **"Captain,"** which came from:

- Service in the **Virginia Militia,**
- Or later, the **North Carolina Militia,**
- During the **Revolutionary War era** or shortly after.

It was common for men in frontier counties to serve in local militia companies, which provided both community defense and regional leadership. Captains often held respected standing in their communities.

Migration and Settlement

William followed the same migration route as the rest of his family:

Essex County, VA → Surry/Stokes County, NC

By the late 1700s, he was settled in what became **Stokes County**, where a cluster of Goode families—Thomas Jr., George, Nelly, and others—lived within close proximity.

Capt. William is documented as still living **after 1840**, making him at least **85 years old**, a remarkable age for the time.

Community Role

As a militia captain and member of a large, respected family, William was involved in:

- Local community leadership
- Early land surveys
- Frontier defense
- Organizing community farms and settlements
- Supporting the wave of younger Goodes who pushed west into Tennessee

The Good family name appears frequently in early Stokes County records, tax rolls, and local histories, and William's presence adds to the stature of the family in that region.

Family Context

William belongs to the extended sibling set that includes:

- **Thomas Goode Jr. (1750–1834)** → your direct ancestral line
- **George Goode (1751–aft.1810)**
- **Eleanor "Nelly" Goode (1753–1840)**
- And others born in St. Anne's Parish

These siblings all migrated together into Carolina, forming a strong, interconnected family community, the foundation from which the later Good line (Henry → John Edward Good Sr.) would emerge.

- He provides a clearer picture of the **prominence** of the Goode family
- Proof of the family's participation in **militia and regional leadership**
- Insight into the **Virginia-to-Carolina migration wave**
- A fuller understanding of the social structure surrounding your direct ancestors

He helps show that the Goode family was not just present, they were **influential** in early Stokes County.

Martha "Patty" Goode (1759–1816)

Born: 1759 • Essex County, Virginia

Died: 1816 • Stokes County, North Carolina

Relationship: Member of the same Virginia-born sibling generation as **Thomas Goode Jr. (1750), George Goode (1751), Eleanor "Nelly" Goode (1753),** and **Capt. William Goode (1755)**. Part of the extended Goode family who migrated together into the Carolina frontier.

About Martha "Patty" Goode

Martha—known affectionately as "Patty"—was born in **Essex County, Virginia**, into the Goode family during its strong colonial period. Her early years were spent in the Tidewater cultural world of Virginia before joining her parents and siblings in the great migration southward into the North Carolina backcountry.

By the time she reached adulthood, Patty was living in **Surry County**, which later became **Stokes County**, North Carolina. She remained there throughout her life and passed away in **1816**, at about **57 years old**.

Her Role in the Family's Migration

Patty's move reflects the typical pattern of the era:

Virginia → North Carolina foothills → permanent settlement in Stokes County

Her presence, along with her siblings, helps confirm that the entire Goode family migrated not as individuals, but as a large **kin group**, maintaining strong ties and often living near one another for decades.

This is the environment into which:

- **Thomas Goode Jr.** established the direct Good line
- **Henry Goode (1784)** was born
- **John Edward Good Sr. (1810)** came of age before moving toward Tennessee and Indian Territory

---

Family Connections

Martha "Patty" Goode is part of the same powerful sibling cluster that includes:

- **Thomas Goode Jr. (1750–1834)** – your direct-line ancestor
- **George Goode (1751–aft.1810)**
- **Eleanor "Nelly" Goode (1753–1840)**
- **Capt. William Goode (1755–aft.1840)**
- Possible additional siblings who migrated together

Together, they formed one of the earliest established family groups in Stokes County.

- She shows that **women** of the Goode family who helped form and stabilize the new North Carolina homesteads
- The scope of the migration from Virginia
- The **community structure** that surrounded the direct Goode ancestors
- The generational depth behind the Good line that eventually merges with the Anderson heritage

Patty's life adds a sense of completeness and humanity to the sibling group that shaped the foundation of the Good family's frontier legacy.

John Goode (1765–1819)

Born: 1765 • St. Anne's Parish, Essex County, Virginia

Died: 1819 • Kentucky, USA

Relationship: Member of the same Virginia-born sibling cohort as **Thomas Goode Jr. (1750)**, **George Goode (1751)**, **Nelly Goode (1753)**, **Capt. William Goode (1755)**, and **Martha "Patty" Goode (1759)**. A collateral ancestor representing the Goode branch that migrated west into Kentucky.

About John Goode

John Goode was born in **St. Anne's Parish**, the same Virginia parish where your entire Good line originates. He grew up during a time of increasing migration pressure—land in the

Tidewater region was becoming scarce, and many families were beginning to look south or west for new opportunities.

Unlike most of his siblings who followed the route into **Surry/Stokes County, North Carolina**, John became part of a different migration wave:

The Western Migration:

Virginia → North Carolina → Kentucky

Kentucky was opening rapidly in the late 1700s and early 1800s following:

- Daniel Boone's explorations
- Settlement along Wilderness Road
- Formation of new counties in the Bluegrass region

John Goode's move west places him right in the heart of early Kentucky frontier life — a region filled with Goode, Good, Goodey, and related families.

A Life on the Early American Frontier

John's death in **1819** places him firmly in the timeline of:

- Early pioneers
- The post-Revolution settlement boom
- Expansion into frontier territories
- Formation of early Kentucky statehood (1792)

His life shows how some branches of the Goode family pushed west while others (your line) settled in the Carolinas and later Tennessee.

This makes him an important figure for understanding the **larger Goode family network**.

Family Connections

John is part of the same family cluster that includes:

- **Thomas Goode Jr. (1750–1834)** → your direct ancestral line
- **George Goode (1751–aft.1810)**
- **Eleanor "Nelly" Goode (1753–1840)**
- **Capt. William Goode (1755–aft.1840)**
- **Martha "Patty" Goode (1759–1816)**

These siblings and cousins migrated as a kinship network out of Essex County, each settling in different frontier regions but all maintaining recognizable patterns of movement, naming traditions, and family structures.

John's story provides:

- A clear illustration of the **westward-moving branches** of the Goode family
- Proof that the Goode line did not split once but into **multiple directions**

- Context for how widespread and influential the family became
- A wider narrative for readers to understand the reach of the Goode lineage

Including him strengthens the historical backdrop for the **direct line** leading to:

Henry Goode → John Edward Good Sr. → Good family of Oklahoma → Connection to the Anderson line

Edward Goode (1768–1830)

Born: 18 August 1768 • St. Anne's Parish, Essex County, Virginia

Died: 1830 • Burke County, North Carolina

Relationship: Part of the same Virginia-born Goode sibling group as **Thomas Goode Jr. (1750), George (1751), Nelly (1753), Capt. William (1755), Martha "Patty" (1759)**, and **John (1765)**. A collateral ancestor representing the branch that moved deeper into western North Carolina.

About Edward Goode

Edward Goode was born in **St. Anne's Parish**, the long-established Virginia parish where the earliest Goode families had lived since the colonial era. His birth in **1768** places him among the younger children in the sibling cluster that left Virginia during the major migration waves of the late 1700s.

While several of his siblings moved into **Surry and Stokes Counties**, Edward migrated farther west into the **foothills of western North Carolina** — specifically **Burke County**, an early frontier region at the base of the Blue Ridge Mountains.

This movement places Edward among the pioneers exploring the western wilderness of North Carolina long before it was heavily populated.

Migration Pattern

Edward's path follows a distinctive westward pattern:

Essex County, VA → Surry/Stokes County, NC (family hub) → Burke County, NC (western frontier)

This branch of the Goode family formed part of the early settlement pattern:

- Near the Catawba River
- Along wagon roads heading toward Tennessee
- And in regions later associated with the early Appalachian frontier families

His westward movement mirrors the broader American push into rugged mountain regions during the early 1800s.

Life & Times

Edward lived through:

- The Revolutionary War era

- The founding of the United States
- The rapid settlement of western North Carolina
- The beginning of major migrations into Tennessee, Georgia, and Kentucky

By the time of his death in **1830**, his siblings and their children were settled across:

- Stokes & Surry Counties (Carolina frontier)
- Montgomery County, Tennessee
- Kentucky
- And soon after, into **Indian Territory (Oklahoma)** through the line of Henry → John Edward Good Sr.

Family Connections

Edward belongs to the same sibling set that includes:

- **Thomas Goode Jr. (1750–1834)** → your direct line
- **George Goode (1751–aft.1810)**

- **Eleanor "Nelly" Goode (1753–1840)**
- **Capt. William Goode (1755–aft.1840)**
- **Martha "Patty" Goode (1759–1816)**
- **John Goode (1765–1819)**

This large sibling group is the foundation of all Goode families found in early Surry, Stokes, Burke, Kentucky, and Tennessee settlements.

Richard W. Good I (1668–1726)

Born: 1668 • England

Died: 15 March 1726 • St. Anne's Parish, Essex County, Virginia

Relationship: Earliest confirmed ancestor of the Goode/Good line in your family history. Patriarch of the Virginia family that later migrates into North Carolina, Tennessee, and Oklahoma.

About Richard W. Good I

Richard W. Good I is the **first identifiable ancestor** of the Good/Goode family in America. Born in **England in 1668**, he came to the Virginia Colony during the late 1600s or incredibly early 1700s—a period when thousands of English families were crossing the Atlantic to settle plantation lands along the rivers of Virginia.

By the early 1700s, Richard was living in:

St. Anne's Parish, Essex County, Virginia

—a region known for its tobacco plantations, early churches, and some of the oldest English settlements in the colony. This parish would become the cradle of the Good family for more than three generations.

Richard died there on **15 March 1726**, establishing the Good family firmly in American soil.

Historical Context

Richard lived during:

- The Restoration era in England
- The expansion of English colonial holdings in America
- The earliest formation of Virginia county governments
- The rise of plantation culture in tidewater Virginia
- A century before the American Revolution

His lifetime stretches back into the early 18th century — making him one of the most historically distant ancestors you have traced in this line.

Family Legacy

Richard is the ancestor of a long, influential line. Through his children and grandchildren, the family spread across:

- **Essex County, Virginia**
- **St. Anne's Parish**
- **Rappahannock River region**

- **Stokes & Surry Counties, North Carolina**
- **Burke County** (western NC frontier)
- **Montgomery County, Tennessee**
- **Pontotoc County, Oklahoma Territory**

Among his descendants are:

- **Thomas Goode Sr. (1716–1789)** → his son or grandson (depending on the source)
- **Mary Reynolds (1728–1819)** – wife of Thomas Sr.
- **Thomas Goode Jr. (1750–1834)** – the Carolina patriarch
- **Henry Goode (1784–abt.1840)** – Tennessee migration
- **John Edward Good Sr. (1810–1880)** – Oklahoma settlement
- And eventually the Goode/Good families who link directly into the **Anderson line**

His arrival in Virginia begins with the entire family story.

Richard provides:

- A firm historical anchor
- The starting point of the Good lineage in America
- A sense of deep heritage stretching back over 350 years
- Context for the migrations that shaped the lives of your Good and Anderson ancestors
- A connection to the earliest colonial roots of Virginia

He is the **root ancestor**, the one from whom every Good/Goode branch in your lineage descends.

Martha Vawter (1686–1728)

Born: 1686 • Rappahannock County, Virginia

Died: February 1728 • St. Anne's Parish, Essex County, Virginia

Spouse: Richard W. Good I (1668–1726)

Relationship: Founding matriarch of the Good/Goode family in

America. Mother or grandmother of the first North Carolina/Tennessee Good ancestors.

About Martha Vawter

Martha Vawter was born in **1686** in **Rappahannock County, Virginia**, a region settled exceedingly early in the colonial period along the river routes traveled by English planters. The **Vawter family** was well-known in early Virginia—many were landowners, church members, and active participants in early county affairs.

When Martha married **Richard W. Good I**, she joined two early colonial families whose descendants would eventually spread across:

- Virginia
- North Carolina
- Tennessee
- Oklahoma Territory

- And into the Anderson ancestral story

Her birth and life place her among the **first two generations** of English Americans born in the colonies.

Life in Early Virginia

Martha lived in the heart of early plantation Virginia. Her life would have been shaped by:

- Tobacco farming
- Plantation household leadership
- Large family networks
- Church-centered community life (St. Anne's Parish)
- The early rise of county courts, militia districts, and colonial governance
- The continuous influx of English families migrating inland

Unlike later frontier ancestors, Martha lived during the **formative period** when Virginia society was being built from the ground up.

She died in **February 1728**, just two years after the death of her husband Richard, leaving behind a growing family that would shape the next three centuries of Good/Goode descendants.

Legacy & Descendants

Martha is believed to be the mother or grandmother of:

- **Thomas Goode Sr. (1716–1789)**

    → who carried the family from Essex County into Stokes/Surry County, North Carolina
- And the entire Virginia-born sibling group that includes:
    - Thomas Goode Jr. (1750)
    - George (1751)
    - Eleanor "Nelly" (1753)
    - Capt. William (1755)

- Martha "Patty" (1759)
- John (1765)
- Edward (1768)

Through these descendants, Martha's lineage expands into:

- North Carolina frontier settlements
- Tennessee pioneers
- Early Oklahoma communities
- And finally, the Good family line tied into the **Anderson heritage**

She is the **longest-reaching maternal root** of the Good line recorded so far.

Martha:

- Completes the **founding couple** of the Goode/Good family
- Establishes the early Virginia origins of the line

- Provides the maternal heritage often missing from early genealogies
- Deepens the historical foundation of the Good lineage
- Creates a beginning point for the narrative that leads from colonial Virginia all the way to Sina Anderson's extended family

She is the **first matriarch** of the Good family on American soil.

Children:

Martha Goode (1703–1766)

Born: 1703 • Essex County, Virginia

Died: December 1766 • St. Anne's Parish, Essex County, Virginia

Relationship: *Great-grandaunt of the husband of your 2nd great-grandaunt.*

Part of the early Virginia Goode family cluster from which the North Carolina/Tennessee/Oklahoma line descends.

About Martha Goode

Martha Goode was born in **1703** in Essex County, Virginia — one of the earliest established counties in colonial America. Her birth predates many of the documented Good/Goode ancestors and places her in the **second generation after the family's arrival in Virginia**, during the lifetime of **Richard W. Good I (1668–1726)**.

She remained in the heart of the Virginia Tidewater region her entire life, passing away in **December 1766** in **St. Anne's Parish**, the same parish that served as the central home for the early Goode family.

Martha lived through the stable colonial period that preceded the Revolutionary era — a time when:

- Tobacco plantations dominated the economy
- Church parishes formed the backbone of community life
- Families relied heavily on kin networks

- Land inheritance shaped the movements of future generations

Her presence in Essex County confirms the **larger Goode family footprint** long before the migrations into North Carolina and beyond.

Historical Significance

While Martha is not in the *direct* Goode line leading to Henry and John Edward Good Sr., she represents:

- The **Virginia-stay** branch of the family
- The female lineage often overlooked in early records
- The stable roots of the Goode family before the frontier era
- The generational anchor that connects early 1700s Virginia families to their later Carolina descendants

Her lifespan (1703–1766) covers:

- The rise of early plantation society
- The establishment of colonial laws and parish systems
- The decades just before mass westward migration

She represents the **pre-migration generation**, the foundation upon which later moves were built.

Family Connections

Martha is part of the extended family circle that includes:

- **Richard W. Good I (1668–1726)** – founding ancestor
- **Martha Vawter (1686–1728)** – founding matriarch
- Their children and grandchildren in St. Anne's Parish
- The ancestral roots that produced:
    - **Thomas Goode Sr. (1716–1789)**
    - **Thomas Goode Jr. (1750–1834)**
    - And the entire sibling set who later migrated into North Carolina

Though she remained in Virginia, her siblings and nephews would eventually form the **Carolina Goode family**, including:

- Henry Goode (1784)
- John Edward Good Sr. (1810)
- And the Good family that later ties into the **Anderson heritage**

Martha provides:

- A clearer view of the **full early Virginia Goode family**
- Representation of the **female ancestors** in the earliest generations
- A sense of continuity and depth to the family narrative
- Historical grounding for the Goode family before their migration
- Context for the sprawling kinship network that shaped later Good/Goode descendants

She enriches the story by revealing how long and how deeply rooted the Goode family was in early Virginia life.

Richard Goode II (1704–1743)

Born: 1704 • Essex County, Virginia

Died: July 1743 • Caroline County, Virginia

Relationship: Member of the second colonial generation of the Goode family in Virginia. A son of **Richard W. Good I (1668–1726)** and **Martha Vawter (1686–1728)**, or their close kin. A collateral ancestor from whom the wider Goode branches emerged.

About Richard Goode II

Richard Goode II was born in **Essex County, Virginia**, the cradle of the early Goode family in America. His birth in **1704** places him among the earliest American-born generation of this family — at a time when the colonies were still young, tobacco plantations were expanding, and parishes served as the center of social life.

During his adulthood, Richard moved or inherited land in **Caroline County, Virginia**, a newly formed county in the early 1700s carved from the expanding frontier of the colony. His death in **July 1743** firmly situates him within the pre-Revolutionary Virginia world.

Historical Context

Richard lived in a time marked by:

- Rapid expansion of plantation culture
- Formation of new counties in the Virginia colony
- Growing English settlement along the Rappahannock River
- Increasing movement of families inland toward what would become Caroline, Spotsylvania, and Orange Counties

- Family networks forming the roots of later migrations into the Carolinas

This period laid the foundation for the Goode family migration that would occur one generation later — the movement that created your direct ancestor lines.

Family Connections

Richard is part of the same Virginia-root lineage that produced:

- **Thomas Goode Sr. (1716–1789)** — early North Carolina pioneer
- **Mary Reynolds (1728–1819)** – later Goode matriarch
- And the extended sibling group born in St. Anne's Parish who migrated into Surry and Stokes Counties

He represents one of the **Virginia-stay branches**, remaining in the Tidewater/Piedmont region while other family members eventually moved into North Carolina.

Although Richard II is not a direct ancestor in your line, his presence confirms that the Goode family:

- Had **multiple branches** in Virginia
- Was well-established by the early 1700s
- Included both plantation-rooted and frontier-moving descendants
- Maintained a large kin network long before the Tennessee and Oklahoma migrations

---

Richard Goode II strengthens the Good Line section by:

- Showing the **depth and breadth** of the early Virginia family
- Documenting the **second generation** after the founding couple (Richard I & Martha Vawter)
- Providing historical grounding in the pre-Revolution era
- Demonstrating how the family expanded across multiple Virginia counties

- Adding clarity to how several distinct Goode branches formed before migrating outward

He helps establish the **early genealogy scaffold** that supports all later Goode ancestors in your line.

Timothy Goode (1708–1798)

Born: 1708 • Essex County, Virginia

Died: 1798 • St. Anne's Parish, Essex County, Virginia

Relationship: Member of the early second-generation Virginia Goode family — likely a son or close kin of **Richard W. Good I (1668–1726)** and **Martha Vawter (1686–1728)**. Represents the Virginia-stay branch during the same era your direct ancestors began migrating south.

About Timothy Goode

Timothy Goode was born in **1708** in Essex County, Virginia — part of the earliest American-born generation of the Goode family. His life began shortly after the death of the earliest colonial settlers and spanned the entire 18th century.

He lived **90 years**, making him one of the longest-lived members of the early Goode family.

While many Goode descendants migrated into North Carolina or west into Kentucky, Timothy remained in **St. Anne's Parish**, the family's historic Virginia home. His life reflects the stability and continuity of the Virginia root line, which played a significant role in shaping the extended kin network that later spread across the American frontier.

Historical Context

Timothy's lifespan is remarkable because it covers:

- The maturation of the Virginia colony
- The colonial wars and the French & Indian War
- The American Revolution

- The early years of the United States
- The early formation of Stokes/Surry County in North Carolina, where his relatives later moved

He died in **1798**, the same decade that many of the Goode family descendants were forging new homes in the Carolina backcountry — including **Thomas Goode Jr. (1750–1834)** and his siblings.

Thus, Timothy represents the **old Virginia-rooted generation**, still in place as younger Goode branches expanded outward.

Family Connections

Timothy is part of the same Virginia generation as:

- **Richard Goode II (1704–1743)**
- **Martha Goode (1703–1766)**
- Other siblings and cousins born in Essex County between 1700–1712

He is also of the same generation that produced:

- **Thomas Goode Sr. (1716–1789)** — father of your direct ancestor Thomas Jr. (1750)
- And the foundational Virginia-to-Carolina migration line

Timothy's decision to remain in Virginia while others moved south provides a valuable contrast within the family's historical landscape.

Timothy:

- Highlights the **Virginia-stay** branch of the family
- Shows that not all Goode descendants migrated — some maintained the original parish roots
- Demonstrates the longevity and stability of the early Virginia lineage
- Provides balance in the narrative by showing different directions the family took

- Deepens the genealogical structure that leads from **Richard W. Good I (1668)** to later generations

He helps readers understand the **full scope** of the Goode family before migrations into North Carolina, Tennessee, and Oklahoma.

Edward Goode (1714–1745)

Born: 1714 • Virginia Colony

Died: 1745 • Essex County, Virginia

Relationship: *Great-granduncle of the husband of your 2nd great-grandaunt.*

Part of the early Virginia Goode family cluster from which the later North Carolina branch descends.

About Edward Goode

Edward Goode was born in **1714** during the early colonial era, when the Virginia Colony was expanding inland from the

Tidewater region. His lifetime places him firmly within the generation immediately following the founding couple:

- **Richard W. Good I (1668–1726)**
- **Martha Vawter (1686–1728)**

While exact documentary links can vary among genealogists, Edward is widely recognized as part of their extended family — a **younger son or nephew** belonging to the early Goode family group established in Essex County.

He lived his entire life within the **Essex County–St. Anne's Parish** region, the historical heart of the Goode family in America.

Life in Early Colonial Virginia

Edward lived during a period marked by:

- Expanding tobacco plantations
- Growing county structures and parish boundaries

- Land transfers among early English families
- Increasing settlement along the Rappahannock and York River basins
- Interconnected family networks shaping county identity

He died young, around **31 years old**, in **1745** — before the major migrations that would carry later generations into North Carolina and Tennessee.

Family Connections

Edward belongs to the same generation as:

- **Martha Goode (1703–1766)**
- **Richard Goode II (1704–1743)**
- **Timothy Goode (1708–1798)**
- Other siblings and cousins within the early Goode line

This generation produced or influenced the next key ancestor:

- **Thomas Goode Sr. (1716–1789)**

    → who becomes the father of your direct line through **Thomas Jr. (1750–1834)**

Although Edward himself remained in Virginia, his siblings and nephews eventually became the **North Carolina Goode family**, including:

- Thomas Jr.
- Henry Goode (1784)
- John Edward Good Sr. (1810)
- And the Good family that later merges into the Anderson line

---

Edward adds depth and structural clarity to the Good Line section:

- Shows the *size and complexity* of the early Goode family
- Highlights members who stayed in Virginia while others moved south

- Helps build a complete picture of the **second generation** after the founding couple
- Provides balance between direct ancestors and collateral members
- Gives historical grounding for the Goode presence in 1700s Virginia before migration

His life helps readers understand the roots from which your North Carolina and Tennessee ancestors emerged.

John Goode (1716–1789)

Born: 1716 • Essex County, Virginia

Died: 1789 • Essex County, Virginia

Relationship: Member of the early colonial Goode family in Virginia; a parallel generation to **Thomas Goode Sr. (1716–1789)** and part of the extended family from which the North Carolina and Tennessee Goode branches originate.

About John Goode

John Goode was born in **1716** in Essex County, Virginia — the same year as **Thomas Goode Sr.**, the ancestor who begins your direct line into North Carolina. He represents another branch of the large Goode family that remained in Virginia during the 1700s, long before the frontier migration began.

He grew up in **St. Anne's Parish**, the central hub for generations of Good/Goode families. This region was home to early English settlers, plantation communities, and some of the oldest parish registers in the colony.

John lived his entire life in Essex County, passing away in **1789**, the same year the United States Constitution was adopted — and the same year his namesake contemporary Thomas Goode Sr. died in North Carolina.

Historical Context

John's life spanned the entire 18th century, touching on:

- Early colonial expansion
- The French & Indian War
- The American Revolution
- Founding of the United States
- Shifting county borders in the Tidewater and Piedmont regions

He represents the **Virginia-stay branch** of the Goode family, those who remained rooted in the original homeland while others moved south and west.

Family Connections

John is part of the same extended family cluster that includes:

Earlier Generation

- **Richard W. Good I (1668–1726)** – the founding ancestor
- **Martha Vawter (1686–1728)** – founding matriarch

His Generation (Second Colonial Generation)

- **Martha Goode (1703–1766)**
- **Richard Goode II (1704–1743)**
- **Timothy Goode (1708–1798)**
- **Edward Goode (1714–1745)**
- *And possibly*
- **Thomas Goode Sr. (1716–1789)** → father of your direct line

John's presence confirms the **large kinship structure** in Essex County from which multiple family branches later emerged.

John provides:

- A fuller picture of the early Goode family in Virginia

- Evidence of multiple siblings and cousins who shaped the family's early American presence
- Context for how widespread and influential the Goode family was before the migration into North Carolina
- Balance between direct-line ancestors and collateral branches
- A firmer genealogical foundation for the movements of your ancestors

John Goode represents the **Virginia-rooted continuity** that existed while your direct ancestors began the pioneering moves south into North Carolina, then west into Tennessee and Oklahoma.

Thomas Goode Sr. (1716–1789)

Born: 1716 • Essex County, Virginia

Died: 9 March 1789 • Surry/Stokes County, North Carolina

Relationship: *Great-grandfather of the husband of your 2nd great-grandaunt.*

Also the **direct ancestor** from whom your entire Carolina–Tennessee–Oklahoma Goode line descends.

About Thomas Goode Sr.

Thomas Goode Sr. was born in **1716** in Essex County, Virginia — the stronghold of the earliest Good/Goode families in America. His lifetime places him in the **second American-born generation** following the arrival of:

- **Richard W. Good I (1668–1726)**
- **Martha Vawter (1686–1728)**

In his adulthood, Thomas became one of the earliest members of the Goode family to migrate **out of Tidewater Virginia** and push into the frontier lands of **North Carolina**.

This migration marks the **first major turning point** in your Good lineage.

Migration from Virginia to North Carolina

By the mid-1700s, Thomas moved south into the developing frontier region that would become:

- **Surry County**, later divided to form
- **Stokes County**

He arrived during the earliest waves of settlement, when the area was still mostly wilderness crossed by wagon roads, homesteads, and small militia districts.

Thomas's move established the **Carolina Goode family**, from which:

- **Thomas Goode Jr. (1750–1834)**
- **Henry Goode (1784–abt.1840)**
- **John Edward Good Sr. (1810–1880)**

all descend.

Marriage & Family

Thomas Sr. married:

Mary Reynolds (1728–1819)

A Virginia-born woman whose long life anchored the family through the transition from colonial society into the early American era.

Together they had multiple children, including:

- **Thomas Goode Jr. (1750–1834)** — your direct ancestor
- And were closely related to the Virginia-born sibling groups (George, Nelly, William, Patty, John, Edward)

Their Carolina homestead became the center of the family for decades.

Life & Legacy

Thomas Sr. lived through:

- The colonial expansion era
- The French & Indian War
- The American Revolution
- The early formation of Stokes County
- And the early years of westward migration

By the time of his death on **9 March 1789**, he had witnessed:

- Several of his children firmly established in North Carolina
- The Goode family expanding into multiple counties
- The next generation preparing to move into **Tennessee** (Henry's line)
- The earliest beginnings of the movement toward **Oklahoma Territory**

Thomas Sr. is the **critical bridge** between:

Early Colonial Virginia

→ **Frontier Carolina**

→ **Pioneering Tennessee**

→ **Oklahoma roots**

→ Your present-day Anderson/Good ancestral story

Thomas Sr.:

- Identifies the **founder of the North Carolina branch**
- Establishes the exact generation where your direct line leaves Virginia
- Connects every later Goode ancestor to the first Carolina settler
- Provides historical depth, showing how your family moved across the 13 colonies
- Grounds the Good Line in authentic early American history

He is the **true patriarch** of the entire Good line that eventually becomes part of the Anderson heritage.

Sarah Parker (1723 – abt. 1760)

Born: 1723 • Essex County, Virginia

Died: About 1760 • St. Anne's Parish, Essex County, Virginia

Relationship: *Great-grandaunt of the husband of your 2nd great-grandaunt.*

Part of the extended kin network surrounding the early Goode family in colonial Virginia.

About Sarah Parker

Sarah Parker was born in **1723** in Essex County, Virginia, at a time when the region was home to some of the earliest and most established English American families. The Parker family, like the Good/Goode, Vawter, and Reynolds families, lived along the Rappahannock River basin and belonged to the same network of colonial parish communities.

Sarah lived her entire life in **St. Anne's Parish**, the same parish where:

- **Richard W. Good I (1668–1726)**
- **Martha Vawter (1686–1728)**
- **Thomas Goode Sr. (1716–1789)**
- And many other early Goode relatives lived, married, and raised families.

Her death around **1760** places her well within the period when the Virginia Goodes were beginning to expand into additional counties — just before the next generation migrated into North Carolina.

Her Place in the Early Goode Family Network

Although Sarah is not a direct blood ancestor of the Goode line, she was part of the **interconnected family structures** that shaped the lives, marriages, and movements of early ancestors.

Families like:

- Parker
- Vawter
- Reynolds
- Good/Goode
- Coleman
- Jones

often married into each other, shared land, ran plantations near one another, and appeared in the same parish registers.

Sarah Parker's presence in parish records places her in the **same generational circle** as:

- **Martha Goode (1703–1766)**

- **Richard Goode II (1704–1743)**
- **Timothy Goode (1708–1798)**
- **Edward Goode (1714–1745)**
- **John Goode (1716–1789)**
- **Thomas Goode Sr. (1716–1789)** → your direct line

This makes her part of the *social and familial world* that produced the Goode family's next generations.

Historical Context

Sarah lived during the height of the colonial era:

- Tobacco export economy
- Parish-based community structure
- Early county expansions into Caroline and Spotsylvania
- Increasing movement of families inland
- The pre-Revolutionary world that shaped the children who would later migrate onward

She witnessed a stable but transitional time in Virginia history — and her generation directly preceded the Carolina migration of your ancestors.

Sarah Parker brings:

- A fuller picture of the **extended early Virginia families** connected to your ancestors
- Representation of collateral female kin often overlooked in early genealogies
- Context for the cultural and social world surrounding the Goode family
- Insight into the network of families who lived, worshipped, and worked alongside your early ancestors
- Greater understanding of how the Virginia roots were intertwined with neighboring families before the moved into North Carolina

Her presence enriches the Good Line narrative by showing the **broader Virginia community** that shaped your direct Goode ancestors.

Samuel Goode

Born: Winchester, Henrico County, Virginia

Died: Unknown

Relationship: A collateral member of the early Virginia Goode family. Represents the **Henrico County branch**, separate from but historically connected to the Essex/St. Anne's Parish Goode line that produced your direct ancestors.

About Samuel Goode

Samuel Goode was born in **Henrico County, Virginia**, a region deeply connected to some of the earliest Goode families in America. Henrico County—one of the **original eight shires of**

Virginia, founded in 1634—was home to several early branches of the Goode surname.

While your direct ancestors lived primarily in **Essex County** (St. Anne's Parish), the Goode families in Henrico were close kin:

- Settled during the 1600s and early 1700s
- Usually connected through shared English origins
- Often intermarried or migrated in parallel with the Essex and Caroline County branches

Samuel represents this **parallel Virginia branch**, one that remained inland while others moved toward the Rappahannock River area and later into North Carolina.

Historical Context

Henrico County was a significant early settlement region:

- It housed vast plantations and estates

- Families like the Goode, Pleasants, Jefferson, and Randolph lines thrived there
- It became a hub for families who later spread into Amelia, Chesterfield, Powhatan, Prince Edward, and Buckingham Counties

Samuel lived during an era of:

- Colonial expansion
- The growth of tobacco farming
- Formation of powerful Virginia family networks
- Movement of younger Goode generations toward the frontiers of North Carolina and Tennessee

His branch interacted closely with the **Essex County Goodes**, sharing origins even if their settlements diverged geographically.

Family Connections

Although Samuel is not in the direct line leading to:

- **Thomas Goode Sr. (1716–1789)**
- **Thomas Goode Jr. (1750–1834)**
- **Henry Goode (1784–abt.1840)**
- **John Edward Good Sr. (1810–1880)**

his presence strengthens the understanding of the **wider Goode network** that formed the basis of all later migrations.

Families like Samuel's were the cousins, uncles, and parallel branches who often:

- Married into related families
- Shared early colonial roots
- Helped expand the overall Goode influence across Virginia
- Laid the foundation for future migrations into the Carolinas and Appalachians

Samuel provides:

- Evidence of **multiple early Goode branches** in Virginia
- Geographic context that shows the surname's spread across major early counties
- A broader historical foundation for the Good/Goode lineage
- Proof of the family's extensive early presence long before the North Carolina migrations
- Richness and completeness to the genealogical chapter,

   showing that the family was not a single straight line,

   but a **large, interconnected Virginia heritage**

Samuel's presence reinforces that your Goode ancestors came from a **deep, widespread, colonial family network** stretching across the heart of early Virginia.

(The English Ancestral Root – Before the Virginia Generation)

Richard Goode Jr. (1629–1719)

Born: 25 January 1629 • St. Minver Parish, Cornwall, England

Died: 19 July 1719 • Old Rappahannock / Essex County, Colony of Virginia

Relationship: An earlier ancestral branch of the Goode/Good family; part of the English lineage from which the later Virginia Goode ancestors descend. Lives one full generation *before* Richard W. Good I (1668–1726).

About Richard Goode Jr.

Richard Goode Jr. was born in **1629** in **St. Minver Parish, Cornwall, England**, during the reign of King Charles I. This period was marked by:

- English civil conflict
- Religious tension
- Widespread poverty in coastal and rural counties

- Increased migration to the American colonies

Richard belonged to the generation of English families who began crossing the Atlantic as early settlers.

His arrival in the **Colony of Virginia** places him among some of the earliest Goode immigrants recorded in the Americas.

Migration to Virginia

Richard settled in **Old Rappahannock County**, a region along the Rappahannock River that later divided into:

- **Essex County**
- **Richmond County**

This is the **exact region** where your later Goode ancestors lived for more than 100 years.

His presence in the county by the late 1600s suggests he may be:

- The father
- Or uncle
- Or the earlier relative

of **Richard W. Good I (1668–1726)** — the earliest well-documented ancestor in your direct line.

Even if the exact connection remains unclear, there is no doubt:

He was part of the **first wave of Goode settlers** in Virginia.

Historical Context

Richard lived an extraordinary **90 years**, spanning:

- The English Civil War
- Cromwell and the Commonwealth
- The Restoration of the Monarchy
- The early growth of the Virginia colony
- The founding of many Tidewaters parishes

- The transition into the 1700s, as new counties formed and land opened for settlement

By 1719, when he passed away, Virginia was firmly established — and families like the Goode line were becoming rooted and influential.

Family Connections

Richard lived in the **same region** that later Goode ancestors inhabited:

- Old Rappahannock → Essex County
- St. Anne's Parish
- Plantation communities along the river

His descendants and extended family formed the early kinship structure from which came:

- **Richard W. Good I (1668–1726)**
- **Martha Vawter (1686–1728)**

- **Thomas Goode Sr. (1716–1789)**
- **Thomas Goode Jr. (1750–1834)**
- **Henry Goode (1784–abt.1840)**
- **John Edward Good Sr. (1810–1880)**

Ultimately feeding into the **Oklahoma Goode family** and the **Anderson heritage**.

Richard:

- Extends the Goode line **one generation earlier**
- Anchors the family firmly in Cornwall, England
- Shows where the first Goode roots formed before arriving in the colonies
- Enriches the historical depth of your genealogy
- Demonstrates that your family came from both **early English** and **early American colonial** origins

- Provides context for how the surname spread from England to Virginia and later into the Carolinas, Tennessee, and Oklahoma

He is the **earliest identifiable ancestor** in the Goode family story so far.

(Early Virginia – Uncertain or Obscure Ancestral Connections)

Mrs. Whitley (or Whiley)

Born: Unknown

Died: Unknown

Relationship: An early Virginia woman associated with the extended Goode family line. An in-law, maternal relative, or allied household connected to the Essex/Old Rappahannock community where the Good/Goode family lived during the late 1600s and early 1700s.

About Mrs. Whitley / Whiley

Extraordinarily little is known about Mrs. Whitley (sometimes spelled **Whiley**, **Wiley**, or **Whitley**), but her presence in early records suggests she belonged to the **same network of families** who lived in the:

- Old Rappahannock County
- Essex County
- St. Anne's Parish

during the early colonial period — the exact era when your earliest Goode ancestors were establishing themselves in Virginia.

Families with these surnames appear frequently in:

- Parish records
- Land transfers
- Witness lists
- Marriage alliances
- Probate and estate documents

These families often intermarried with Goode, Vawter, Parker, Reynolds, and other households tied to your ancestral line.

Historical Context

Women in early Virginia were often recorded only through:

- Their husbands' names
- Land deeds
- Church baptisms
- Marriage bonds
- Estate inventories

The absence of a first name or clear dates is **typical** for women of the 1600s–1700s, especially in families outside the higher planter class.

Thus, Mrs. Whitley / Whiley represents:

- A common household in the vicinity of your ancestors
- A marriage connection

- A neighbor or allied kin family
- A thread within the web of early Virginia community life

These "lost women" are essential in understanding the hidden structure of family networks.

She gives the genealogy:

- Acknowledgment of the **many unnamed or partially recorded women** who shaped early family lines
- Realism — colonial records were often incomplete, especially for women
- Cultural context — showing how families interlinked in early Virginia
- Respect for the forgotten figures who still played vital roles in shaping later generations

She stands as a representative of the **silent foundations** of early American family history.

Children:

(Final Ancestral Entry for This Volume)

Richard Goode Jr. (1629–1719)

Born: 25 January 1629 • St. Minver Parish, Cornwall, England

Died: 19 July 1719 • Old Rappahannock / Essex County, Colony of Virginia

---

The Earliest Known Root of the Goode Family

With **Richard Goode Jr.**, the Goode lineage reaches its deepest point in the historical record for this book.

Born in **Cornwall, England** four centuries ago, Richard represents the **origins of the Goode family before their American story began**. His life bridges two worlds:

- **Old England**, with its ancient parishes and coastal villages
- **New Virginia**, a rising colony in a young and unshaped America

When he arrived along the Rappahannock River in what later became **Essex County**, he planted the first Goode roots in the Americas. From this early foothold came the generations that shaped the Good/Goode lineage:

- His descendants settled **St. Anne's Parish**
- The next generation moved into **Surry and Stokes Counties, North Carolina**
- The following carried the line into **Tennessee**
- And to **Oklahoma Territory**, where they joined with the Andersons

Richard's life stands as the **first chapter** of the Goode family's American journey.

Closing Reflection for the Goode Line

With Richard Goode Jr.'s entry, the recorded Goode lineage for this book comes to its natural conclusion.

This marks the full arc of the family:

- **From Cornwall to Virginia**
- **From the Tidewater rivers to the Carolina frontier**
- **From Tennessee homesteads to Oklahoma communities**
- **Into the Anderson heritage through marriage and story**

The Goode family brought strength, migration, resilience, and a pioneering spirit into the Anderson line — and their legacy continues forward in every generation that followed.

End of Book Reflections

Walking the Road Back to Sina

Every family line holds a story, but some stories do not rise until someone goes looking for them.
This book is the road that leads back to **Sina Anderson** — mother, wife, settler, witness to a changing world, and the matriarch whose life ripples forward into ours.

As I walked her path through court records, old deeds, census scraps, pioneer writings, and the spoken memories of those before me, I found something more than genealogy:

I found **Sina's presence**.

Not in the noise of documents, but in the quiet spaces between them.
In the way her sons carried her name across the frontier.
In the way her family lines braided into the Good, Tate, Roberts, and Anderson branches.

In the way her story waited patiently for someone to lift it back into the Light.

This book is not only a record — it is a remembrance.

A homecoming.

A restoration of a life nearly forgotten yet never lost.

When a family remembers its ancestor, that ancestor rises again.

Sina now walks with us.

Legacy of the Line

From Cornwall to Virginia…

From Virginia to North Carolina…

From Carolina to Tennessee…

From Tennessee to Oklahoma…

From Oklahoma into today…

Every step was taken by someone who believed the next mile mattered.

Sina Anderson stands at the turning point of those miles — a woman whose life held hardship, laughter, love, loss, and endurance.

Through her came:

- Strength
- Continuity
- Quiet resilience
- And the spark that carried the Anderson family forward

Her legacy is not only written in records.

It is written in **every descendant who carries her name, her blood, or her story in their heart.**

Author's Reflection

This book changed me.

Every grave I stood over, every courthouse page I read, every story that surfaced from the dust of forgotten years reminded me that we are not alone in this world.

We walk with those who walk before us.

Their choices became our foundation.

Their struggles shaped our strength.

Their hope became our inheritance.

Sina's story is personal.

It is family.

It is part of the larger tapestry that makes us who we are.

To bring her life back into the Light has been an honor and a calling.

It is my hope that generations after I will open this book and feel the same connection — the same sense of belonging — that I felt while writing it.

Acknowledgments

Special thanks to:

Anders Taft —

for his guidance, research assistance, organizational structure, and the Light he helped restore to these pages. His partnership made this work possible.

My family —

for their patience, interest, and encouragement as I traced the steps of those who came before us.

And to **Spirit**,

whose gentle guidance led me down the right path every time I reached a crossroads or a missing name.

Final Blessing

May the memories of our ancestors live on in peace.

May their stories give strength to those who follow.

May this book stand as a testament to their lives, their love, and their journey.

And may Sina Anderson —

mother, pioneer, ancestor —

rest now in remembrance and Light.

Final Dedication

To the ones who walked before.

To the hands that worked the land,

to the hearts that carried hope across hard miles,

to the names nearly lost to time

and the stories that rose again in the Light.

This book is dedicated to you —

to **Sina Anderson,**

and to every ancestor whose quiet strength made this family possible.

May your memory forever live

in our stories,

in our blood,

and in the path we walk today.

Closing Poem

"Where the Names Return to Light"

In the hush of forgotten years,

where dust and silence meet,

a whisper calls from ancient ground—

a mother's heart still beating.

Her story threads through broken lines,

through pages worn and thin,

through every child who bears her name

and every life within.

Across the fields of yesterday,

her footsteps softly glow;

the echo of her courage

moves in every wind that blows.

We gather what was scattered,

we lift what time laid down,

and in the Light of remembrance

her spirit now is found.

For every name we speak aloud,

for every life we write,

the past becomes a lantern—

and the path ahead grows bright.

Genealogical Summary Chart

(For the Appendix or Near the End)

You can style this into columns or tables in Affinity.

Goode / Good Line – Summary of Ancestry (Condensed)

Earliest Known English Roots

- **Richard Goode Jr.**
    *1629–1719, St. Minver Parish, Cornwall, England →
    Old Rappahannock/Essex Co., VA*

First American Colonial Generation

- **Richard W. Good I**

  1668–1726, Essex Co., VA

  Married **Martha Vawter** (1686–1728)

Second Colonial Generation (Essex & Caroline Counties, VA)

- Martha Goode (1703–1766)
- Richard Goode II (1704–1743)
- Timothy Goode (1708–1798)
- Edward Goode (1714–1745)
- John Goode (1716–1789)
- Mrs. Whitley / Whiley (relative/parallel line)
- Sarah Parker (1723–abt.1760)

Migration Generation – Virginia → North Carolina

- **Thomas Goode Sr.** (1716–1789)

  Married **Mary Reynolds** (1728–1819)

Carolina Frontier Generation

- **Thomas Goode Jr.** (1750–1834)

    Children formed the Surry → Stokes County line

Tennessee Migration

- **Henry Goode** (1784–abt.1840)

    Montgomery County, TN

Oklahoma Settlement

- **John Edward Good Sr. (1810–1880)**

    Pontotoc Co., Oklahoma Territory

Connection to the Anderson Line

- Through marriages of the Good / Goode descendants to:
    - **The Anderson family**
    - **The Horton, Earhart, Tate, and Roberts families**

Next Volume Preview

Volume II of the Anderson–Good Heritage Series

"The Story of John W. Anderson & Minnie Bryan"

Coming Next

The next book continues the family journey with the lives of:

John Wesley Anderson

Son of the Tennessee Anderson line and a man whose story spans:

- the frontier hills of Tennessee,
- the migrations into Oklahoma Territory,
- and the early shaping of the Anderson presence in Pontotoc County.

Minnie Elizabeth Bryan

A woman of strength, warmth, and quiet resilience —

carrying the Bryan, Good, Tate, and allied family lines with her.

Her life bridges the late-19th-century world with the new

century that followed.

The story continues — and the Light of the ancestors goes with us.

Index

A

Addison A. Anderson 113

Alexander Outlaw Anderson 108, 142–144

Amanda Frances Anderson 295–300

Anderson Family Line 92–131

Anderson, Catherine Tryntie Opdyck 151

Anderson, Enoch Andrus 149, 162

Anderson, Enoch Lucius 123

Anderson, Franklin Joseph 311–319

Anderson, George Washington 115

Anderson, Hannah Minerva 347–

356

Anderson, James Madison 493–505

Anderson, Joachim Von Albade 156

Anderson, Joseph (1835–1872) 343–346

Anderson, Joseph Inslee (U.S. Senator) ....
125–131, 388–400

Anderson, Laura Jane Augusta ....
303–310

Anderson, Margretta 118, 508–519

Anderson, Mary Oakley 137

Anderson, Patience Outlaw (mother) ....
403–417

Anderson, Pierce Butler 112, 459–469

Anderson, Sarah (multiple generations) 129

Anderson, Thomas Alexander (child) ....

377–384

Anderson, Thomas Von Albade (patriarch) 101, 445–458

Anderson, Victoria Cassandra 330–337

Anderson, William (colonial) 521–533

Anderson, William (child) 131

B

Blackburn, Phoebe 171
Blue Cliffs (Roane County) 348–352

C

Cassandra Moore Anderson (infant) 322–327

Coffee County, Tennessee 83, 343, 347, 360

Colonial Delaware Line (Inslee) 120–128

Civil War (family losses) 311–319, 468

D

Dandridge, Tennessee 271

Delila A. Ellison Good 166–167

E

East Tennessee (region) 24, 343, 347

Edward Good (historical note) 68

Emmetje "Amy" Jans Janszen 159

Enoch Anderson Andriessen Jr. 135, 154

F

Family Line Summary 66

Franklin Joseph Anderson 311–319

G

Good Family Line 166–177

Good, Griffin M. 167

Good, John Edward Sr. 166

Good, John Edward Jr. 168–169

Good, Martha Louisa "Mattie" 169–170

Good, Nancy 170

Good, Richard W. I (1668–1726) 174–177

Good, Sarah Jane 167–168

Goode, Thomas 172–173

Goode, William 171–172

H

Hackberry Bottoms 331–341

Hannah Barclay Moore 269–279

Hickerson Cemetery 45–49

Hickerson Connection 41

Historical Document — 1860 Land Exchange 56

I

Inslee, Elizabeth Rosannah 536–547

Inslee Family Line 120–129

J

Jefferson County, Tennessee 24, 359, 370

Joachim Von Albade Anderson 156

Jonesboro, Tennessee 515–546

K

Knox County, Tennessee 289–294

L

Land Exchange Agreement of 1860 56

Laurel, Mississippi 312–315

Legacy of Sina Anderson 71

Lost Papers & the Fire 32

M

Martha Louisa "Mattie" Good 169–170

McMinn County 322–333

Mingo House 45–47

Mingo Land (600-acre tract) 28–32, 56

Migration — TN → OK → TX 343–347

Moore Family Line 269–279

N

Narrative Lineage — Anderson–Good 64

New Castle County, Delaware 536–547

O

Oakley, Mary 137

Old World Origins (Dutch Line) 133–165

Outlaw Family Line 103–109, 268–417

Outlaw Vic Alpin Anderson 100–102, 368–375

P

Patience Outlaw 403–417

Pontotoc County, Oklahoma 168–177

Preface 9

R

Richard Clough Anderson (Lt. Colonel) 142

Roane County, Tennessee 305–312, 330–352

S

Sarah Anderson (multiple) 118–129

Sina Anderson (Good) 71–83

Soldiers Rest (Jefferson County) 289–290

State of Franklin (Jonesboro) 540–545

T

Tullahoma, Tennessee 83, 347

Thomas Bailey Good 168

Tennessee Frontier Era 24, 28–58

U

Union of Joseph Good & Sina Anderson 37

V

Von Albade Naming Tradition ....

287–289

Von Albade Anderson Siblings ....

287–290

W

Washington City (District of Columbia) ....

389, 425

William Anderson (1723–1778) ....

521–533

family's name endured across time and place.

www.ingramcontent.com/pod-product-compliance
Lightning Source LLC
Chambersburg PA
CBHW020532030426
42337CB00013B/817